10 Irrefutable Proofs of Creation

THE SCIENCE BEHIND OUR WORLD

Bill Seng

Copyright © 2015 Bill Seng

10 Irrefutable Proofs of Creation

All rights reserved.

ISBN: 1508547920
ISBN-13: 978-1508547921

All rights reserved solely by the author. The author guarantees all contents are original and do not infringe upon the legal rights of any other person or work. No part of this book may be reproduced in any form without the permission of the author. The views expressed in this book are not necessarily those of the publisher.

Unless otherwise indicated, Bible quotations are taken from the New International Version (NIV). Copyright © 2009 by Zondervan.

DEDICATION

To my parents, Dr. John and Deb Seng.

CONTENTS

	Acknowledgments	i
I	Introduction	ii
1	The First Law of Thermodynamics	1
2	The Second Law of Thermodynamics	10
3	The Expanding Universe	18
4	The Anthropic Principle	26
5	DNA	35
6	Biological Predestination	46
7	Irreducible Complexity	57
8	Natural Selection	67
9	Proof of the Flood	81
10	Mankind	100
C	Conclusion	106

ACKNOWLEDGMENTS

Thank you, once again, Dr. Gary Staats. I may not have written another book on this subject if it were not for your genuine encouragement and desire to share these truths with the world.

A special thank you for all of the people who are involved in both sides of this debate. The depth of insight created through rational discussion will ultimately benefit mankind. In my research for this book I feel like I have grown to know and love all of you very much.

Introduction

There have been many claims that the belief in evolution is factual and that the belief in a Creator is strictly religious and has no supporting evidence. This book is written to address this problem and to shine light on the truth. I have never been one to accept just any premise thrown my way and this one is no exception. It is assumed that because the majority of scientists believe in evolution, the Big Bang, and other naturalistic explanations for origins, that the debate has been settled. Anybody who objects to the reality of these theories is either a con-artist, stupid, or crazy. It is assumed that there is only one way to interpret the evidence, making theories that invoke evolution irrefutable.

But suppose that, perhaps, a great corruption of the sciences has taken place. It is not an issue as to whether these scientists truly believe what they claim to believe, it is a question of whether or not what they believe in is true. If one bad teaching became popular enough that it progressively became canonized throughout scientific textbooks and classrooms, imagine the sort of distortion it could cause. This is exactly what has happened.

Those who believe in evolution have suppressed the teaching of any other faith-based idea from the science classroom. I do not advocate that religion should be taught in the public classroom, but to teach something as a fact when it is clearly not, coupled with the suppression of the other viewpoints, should be a red flag to both science and educational communities. Data presented in the classroom has bias and beliefs on worldview attached to these teachings. It is impossible to present a worldview without such bias. Currently, the secular ideology goes unchallenged in public classrooms with no resolve in sight. What are we to do about these faith-based ideas being taught from a one-sided perspective to students all over the country?

Can anyone make a case that evidence exists which most certainly suggests that there was a supernatural Creator? Can someone bring forth evidence that proves the existence of the supernatural? In this book, I present ten evidences that do just that. I have used the title, *10 Irrefutable Proofs of Creation,* and although the word *proof* is a very strong word, I use it intentionally. Proof is something that cannot warrant any other explanation. So the statement I make with this title is powerful, but does require clarification.

When I use the word proof, I am not saying that there is no other explanation for the evidence I am presenting. I am simply saying that the evidence is present and that the simplest and most common sense explanation for the evidence requires a spark of the supernatural. I have included Scripture verses to prove that the Bible has addressed some of the matters of origins, which science is just now starting to discover. So that there is no confusion, these verses range from specific to possibly figurative or symbolic. I have presented them as clearly as I can to allow for the Scriptures to be well understood in context.

Approach each chapter with an open mind. Some of the ideas I am proposing are somewhat original, others I am sure you have heard before. Regardless, I find these arguments to be some of the most compelling inside of the creation vs. evolution debate. Who can deny the first law of thermodynamics, the earth's ability to house life, and the existence of the fossils of deep sea creatures on the peaks of mountains? The evidence itself is not in question. The question, again, lies in how to interpret these findings. To arrive at any conclusion outside of a Creator takes much intentionality and hard work.

I have done my best to address both sides of the argument. I am probably not going to represent the opposition as well as they would represent themselves, but I will give their ideas a fair shake against what I am suggesting. I will do the best I can to accurately present their counterarguments. I believe that when the facts are presented the way they appear, without imposing unnecessary assumptions, the creation model is the only logical explanation for the natural world.

Bill Seng

THE FIRST LAW OF THERMODYNAMICS

Through him all things were made; without him nothing was made that has been made. ~John 1:3

To start off this study we take the first logical stop in the realm of scientific observation, namely, the First Law of Thermodynamics. This is called the Law of Conservation of Energy. This law simply states that energy can be neither created nor destroyed. The biochemist Isaac Asimov said of the First Law of Thermodynamics, "This law is considered the most powerful and most fundamental generalization about the universe that scientists have ever been able to make."[1] The BIG question that everyone wants to know is where everything came from. The First Law of Thermodynamics

---

[1] Henry Morris, *The Biblical Basis for Modern Science,* Green Forest, Arkansas: Master Books, 172.

quickly gets passed over in this debate because it has been trivialized. Regardless of how this is done, at the end of the day we still have the problem of "Where did everything come from?"

Even from a theistic perspective this is not an easy question to answer. Yes, we know that "In the beginning God created the heavens and the earth." Yes, we know that he created everything out of nothing. But how did he create everything out of nothing? Where did the material come from which he used to create? How can you take nothing and make something? I do not know that anyone knows the answers to these questions other than to say that God did it regardless. A materialistic explanation runs into just as many problems.

Whether you say that the universe is eternal or had a starting point without God, the First Law of Thermodynamics becomes an incredible nuisance. The materialist who believes that the universe had a starting point must not just explain how everything came from nothing, but also how it came to be for no reason. It seems that the only viable solution to such a problem is to say that the universe is eternal. This concept has changed significantly since it was first proposed. It used to be thought that all of the planets and everything just kind of existed and always have. As we have learned more and more about the universe it appears that such a notion that the universe never changes is false. It is now thought by many that the universe is eternal, but goes through cycles of shrinking and expanding. So, when we refer to the Big Bang, the Big Bang that we are referring to is the last Big Bang that happened. According to this model, there have probably been many Big Bangs. After a certain period of time, the product of the Big Bang condenses back into the point of origin and starts all over again.[2] But what started this cycle and where did this point of origin originate? It is possible that the scientists who believe in such a model are wasting a whole lot of time proposing false theories upon which they build more false theories. Both scenarios ultimately violate the First Law of Thermodynamics, by virtue of which both contain an element of the supernatural. Since I have just broken the supernatural barrier, one of the incredible things about the natural sciences, especially physics, is they provide clarity in defining what is and is not possible in the natural world and the physical universe. With so many over used words it is easy to take the First Law for granted. Let us take a moment and clarify what

---

[2] Danny Faulkner, *Study Says Universe had No Beginning and No Big Bang?* 2015. https://answersingenesis.org/big-bang/study-says-universe-had-no-beginning/ [Accessed April 1, 2015].

constitutes a law, a theory, and a hypothesis according to modern science.

A hypothesis is the starting point for an idea before it becomes a theory. A hypothesis normally starts with some sort of an observation. The observation leads to a statement that tries to explain the observation. Take rain, for example. Clearly, rain is water that falls from the sky. This means that there is water up in the sky. Where does this water in the sky come from? One might make a hypothetical statement like, "the water in the sky is from angels and when the angels spit, it falls down to earth." A hypothetical statement remains as a hypothesis until proper experimentation is done.[3]

A theory solidifies when a known phenomenon is duplicated and the factors within the experiment can help to explain why something happens. The theory of evolution is a grand example of a theory. The theory of evolution proposes change in organisms over time through the mechanism of natural selection. If the hypothesis is true, natural selection should be able to accentuate certain characteristics of the creature being observed inside

---

[3]Science Made Simple, *The Scientific Method by Science Made Simple,* 2014.
http://www.sciencemadesimple.com/scientific_method.html #experiment [Accessed April 1, 2015].

of an experimental environment. This can clearly be observed. If these expressed characteristics can be defined as change, the basis for evolution has been established and it can be considered a real scientific theory. A theory is not set in stone as truth, it is just a very well-tested prediction that consistently explains a phenomenon. A theory does not necessarily prove to be true in every instance[4].

A law is a theory that has been tested so thoroughly with such consistent results that there has never been a known contradiction to its premise. In this case, the First Law of Thermodynamics has never been violated. Energy can be changed into different forms, but it is always there. If energy cannot be created or destroyed, why does anything exist at all? It seems that there cannot be a natural explanation so long as it depends on the laws that currently exist in our universe.

Now, think about this all in relation to the supernatural. What is supernatural? It is a phenomenon that defies the natural laws. I have heard a good number of atheists decry miracles because they cannot be duplicated inside of the

[4] Monica Heger, *What is a Theory?* 2012, http://www.livescience.com/32390-what-is-a-theory.html [Accessed April 1, 2015].

laboratory. I have heard a good number of Christians who have adopted a more materialistic philosophy try to explain miracles naturalistically. Both ideas are absurd. You cannot duplicate a miracle upon your own will. To accomplish such a thing you would need to have a transcendent grasp on the universe, by which you could manipulate matter upon your will without regard for governing laws of the universe. You would need to be God.

Looking at the Bible, what are some of the miracles that are detailed? People are brought back from the dead, water is turned into wine, people walk on water, and storms are calmed by the words of one man. None of these are misunderstandings of natural occurring events. These examples directly defy the laws that govern the natural universe. I am not saying that since they violate the laws of nature that they must be true. I am simply stating that whoever wrote about these miracles had to have known for sure that these were not things that happened naturally. Myths from other cultures invoke supernatural explanations for naturally occurring events. This is a very important difference between a religion that is consistent with the natural world and one that is not. That is also why the question of origins is so difficult.

Examining our three options we have quite a problem. A material starting point for the universe would require a rebellion against the laws of physics. Creation through a divine Being begs the questions of where God came from and how he created something out of nothing. Is that not in defiance of the laws of physics? Our other option is an eternally existing universe. To clarify, when an eternally existing universe is proposed in a modern context, it is not meant as it was thousands of years ago. It used to be thought that the planets and stars and everything inanimate in the universe always existed. We know that such a proposition is highly unlikely and maybe impossible.

An eternal universe would have to exist under certain conditions. For one, it would be eternal only in the sense that it is constantly in transition from one form to another; forever expanding and collapsing on itself. Number two, it would have to defy the same laws of physics that a universe with a beginning would have to defy. It would dodge the limits of the First Law of Thermodynamics but the Second Law would then become a problem. Aside from that, there are all sorts of other rules that would need to be overcome to create the well-structured universe in which we live. Third, this means that there would need to be another Law of which we are currently unaware that would have to suspend the physical laws as we know them in order to allow the magic of the Big Bang to do its stuff.[5]

Some people at this point might be very intrigued at the possibility of an eternally existing universe while others are scoffing and thinking it sounds absurd. It solves the problem of the First Law of Thermodynamics, at least, but it creates some questions that may be impossible to answer. What answer might the theist offer to justify a divine creation instead of a material starting point?

The real question is, "How did God overcome the First Law of Thermodynamics?" The answer might not satisfy everyone, but it is as good of an answer as any to the problems of an eternally existing universe: God created the First Law of Thermodynamics. God did not have to overcome the First Law of Thermodynamics because that Law exists only in the physical universe. If God is supernatural and existed before the universe and before the laws of physics, it would be plausible that as Creator he would not be bound by the laws he created. This does not mean that there is nothing more to be known about how he accomplished such an act, indeed it creates more questions. Unfortunately, just like the problems of an eternally existing universe it may be impossible to ever

---

[5] Bert Thompson, *So Long Eternal Universe; "Hello Beginning, Hello End!"* 2003.

http://www.apologeticspress.org/apcontent.aspx?category=12&article=310

answer such questions. It does, however, solve the problem of how a supernatural creation could get around the First Law of Thermodynamics.

What we must conclude is that the creation of the universe was in one sense or another supernatural because nothing else like its occurrence can be duplicated by nature. Since we have entered into the realm of the supernatural, whether we invoke God or not, it opens up the likelihood that something outside of the universe created the universe. As we continue to examine the nine remaining proofs it will become more and more evident that the best explanation for the creation of matter is the divine
hand of God.

THE SECOND LAW OF THERMODYNAMICS

All men are like grass,
and all their glory is like the flowers of the field;
the grass withers and the flowers fall,
but the word of the Lord stands forever.
~1 Peter 1:24-25

    As previously discussed, a scientific law is something that has been displayed with no known exceptions. After rigorous scrutiny if a theory has endured the fires of intense investigation and has been tried and true in every possible instance, the theory gets canonized as a law. The Second Law of Thermodynamics is one such phenomenon. People in every discipline of science are willing to hang their hats on the truth promoted by the Second Law of Thermodynamics, the Law of Entropy. This law is as undeniable as any truth in the universe and should be seen as definite proof for creation. Why do so many people refuse to see God despite the powerful evidence of the Second Law of Thermodynamics?

This Law states that any system of order will break down into disorder over time. For example, if you observe a rock in the middle of the desert you will notice that it will not become more complex over time under natural conditions. The sun, wind, rain, and other natural stressors will take their toll on the rock until it eventually erodes away to nothing.[6] This is not just true with inanimate objects, but also with organisms. After reaching a certain age, humans start to notice the effects of decay upon their bodies. Their hair loses its pigment and sometimes falls out. Their bones lose density. Their memories are diminished. When an elderly person recalls a more youthful time in his or her life it is often remembered to be better than what it really was because of the drastic changes they have experienced. The Second Law of Thermodynamics is always at work.

Naturally, the Second Law of Thermodynamics seems to eliminate the possibility that the orderly systems of the universe could have emerged through purely material processes. If everything came from something, there had to be a starting

---

[6] Henry Morris, 2008, 173.

point somewhere. The starting point, according to this Law could not be *nothing.* If the universe and life's origins are to be attributed to purely material and natural processes, something complex would have existed before everything else did. In a naturalistic sense this totally eliminates the whole point of searching for an origin because by this logic you truly should never find a starting point to the universe. The Big Bang, the formation of the planets and stars, and the evolution of life should all be ruled as impossibilities according to this Law.

Contrary to this logic, advocates of evolution will often say that the Second Law of Thermodynamics is no problem when it comes to organic life developing from inanimate material. An argument that has been popularized by Richard Dawkins is that the earth is an open system. An open system is one that is able to harness the energy being put into it and constructively use it for its own purposes. So when sunlight and other forms of energy are put into planet earth, the result is not a breakdown of order. Instead, the energy acts as a catalyst for processes that he believes resulted in the formation of life. The problem with this hypothesis is that there is no scientific basis for its claims.[7]

---

[7] Dr. Andy McIntosh, *Just Add Energy...* 2007. https://answersingenesis.org/physics/just-add-energy/ [Accessed April 1, 2015].

Yes, an open system can use energy to accomplish a variety of important functions. I think that one of the hallmark examples of such a process is photosynthesis in plants. Photosynthesis is when plants use the power of the sun to create a chemical form of energy that they store in sugar bonds. The difference is between plants and dry dirt or even water is that plants have a pigment called chlorophyll that captures sunlight and from which organelles called chloroplasts conduct the process of photosynthesis. Dirt and water do not have any specialized mechanisms through which they can harness energy that they receive.

Because there is no evidence that suggests that the earth itself can harness energy why would anyone suggest such an idea? The Second Law of Thermodynamics is one of the most supported observations of any scientific concept. It is well known that receiving mechanisms must already be in place for received energy to be used in a constructive manner.[8] The logic of an atheist proceeds in a manner that suggests that although evolution, on many levels, defies the laws of physics it had to have happened. The only alternative is that there must have been a

---

[8] Dr. Art Susman, http://www.mcc.cmu.ac.th/graduate/Agro723/Reading_Materials/Our_Planet/Planet.html [Accessed April 1, 2015].

supernatural Creator and that cannot be true. Because there is no supernatural Creator and we know that evolution is true, there must be some sort of exception to the evolutionary process when considering the Laws of physics and of nature. So, the only place that evidence exists that evolution can overcome the Laws of physics is in the minds of hopeful atheists.

The Second Law of Thermodynamics plays a unique role within the universe. On one hand, it is the most feared force in the universe. Everything will cease to exist as it currently exists and anything that is living will eventually die and turn into dust. On the other hand, it is one of the greatest blessings in the universe. Without it we may not be able to harness energy. Its existence as a physical law is not just hypothetical. It is a definite reality.

In a lecture that Jim Holt gave on TED (Technology, Entertainment, Design) he proposes a spectrum of possible realities. On end of the spectrum, there is a reality that is defined more or less by absolute chaos and randomness. On the other end exists a universe that is what Plato said is a universe that is as full as it can possibly get. In layman's terms, I think he is referring to a universe of such order that there is no possible way that anything could be different from what it is. Then he proposes that we live in a universe that is a balance between the two. We are not a universe that is so chaotic that nothing can be predicted but we are not a universe in which everything can be predicted. He most certainly was not trying to infer that God exists, but that if he does he is a middle-ground God, just like the middle-ground universe that he proposed. According to Holt, God is mostly benevolent but not very effective. This is an intellectual way of stating his heart is in the right place but he is far from perfect. I disagree with his notion of God, but his thoughts on the universe's existence bare much truth.[9]

One of the qualities of the Laws of Thermodynamics is that they create a certain type of balance in the universe. Where the Second Law states that all things are decaying into a less orderly state, the First Law states that matter can neither be created nor destroyed. The First Law is a Law of order. There is a logical progression from one form of energy to another no matter what happens to the original form of energy. Nothing ever pops into existence or is totally obliterated; everything that exists will eventually become something else. The Second Law, ironically, is a Law of chaos. All things decay into a less orderly state. Where the

---

[9] Jim Holt, *Why Does the Universe Exist?* 2014.
https://www.ted.com/talks/jim_holt_why_does_the_universe_exist?language=en

First Law is about preservation, the Second Law is about destruction. Where the First Law describes the fullness of the universe, the Second Law describes the decay of the universe. When these two Laws are looked at in relation to one another, it appears that we arrive at Jim's conclusion. This universe is neither one of absolute fullness nor absolute chaos, but appears to be in between the two.

When this reality is analyzed, the truth that is uncovered is that this is a universe of incredible order. It is clearly seen that there are two opposing forces working against one another, but the Second Law can never overcome the First Law. Even though all things decay into a less orderly state, nothing ever fades into non-existence. There is something remarkably purposeful behind these Laws. This is where good science needs to be interpreted through the lenses of good theology.

There are people that would suggest that the Second Law of Thermodynamics is a result of Original Sin. After Adam and Eve sinned, all things began to decay. This is an inaccurate picture of the Second Law of Thermodynamics because this Law is also carried out in vital processes of life. When a person eats, digests, and metabolizes food, whatever the person is eating must decompose, digest, and metabolize. This is the Second Law at work. But, what the Bible implies is that death was not prevalent until after Original Sin. So even though the principles of the Second Law were being enacted through a process like digestion, it did not necessarily have an effect on an aging individual. The Second Law, therefore, was only partially or mostly active shortly after creation. To what extent God limited the Second Law of Thermodynamics is unclear and for our purposes we will mostly avoid that topic. After Original Sin, the Second Law was amplified and was applied to all of creation.[10]

Although the Second Law declares that all things will breakdown into a more chaotic state, it creates a definite order within our universe. Between the First and Second Laws an incredible balance is created where all matter will always exist, but that it will forever be changing from one form to another. Genesis provides insight into the original intention of this Law. Ultimately, this Law tells us that the universe was created by God because it prohibits any upward evolution from a less complex state of being to a more complex state of being. The only way around this Law would be to invoke supernatural power, just as it was with the First Law of Thermodynamics.

[10]Tommy Mitchell, *The Second Law of Thermodynamics Began at the Fall,* 2010. https://answersingenesis.org/creationism/arguments-to-avoid/the-second-law-of-thermodynamics-began-at-the-fall/ [Accessed April 1, 2015].

THE EXPANDING UNIVERSE

He sits enthroned above the circle of the earth, and its people are like grasshoppers. He stretches out the heavens like a canopy, and spreads them out like a tent to live in.
~ Isaiah 40:22

It was once thought that the earth was flat and fixed in place. When Christianity was established as a legal religion in Rome, certain Scripture verses were used to support such a notion. Many people later came along and dispelled the idea that the world was flat. Before the rise of Christianity, in 500 B. C. the great Greek mathematician, Pythagoras, made some stunning observations. He noticed that as he observed the moon, its shadow behaved in a manner consistent with spherical objects. He was convinced that the moon was spherical and concluded that the earth must be round as well. One hundred and fifty years later the

Greek philosopher, Aristotle, was observing the movement of the constellations and also came to the conclusion that the world was spherical. Not everyone accepted these conclusions but the knowledge still existed.[11]

Aristotle also undertook the task of determining the earth's relation to the rest of the universe. Looking at the heavens was baffling to him. Considering the limits on technology in his days it is incredible to think that he could have come up with as sophisticated of a model as he did, despite the fact that his conclusions were wrong. He determined that the universe consisted of 55 concentric, crystalline spheres on which the planets were attached. In the middle of the 55 spheres was the earth. So he concluded that the earth was the center of the universe. The spheres moved at a constant velocity and were ultimately under the influence of the outermost sphere known as the *Sphere of the Prime Mover.* About two hundred years later another philosopher/scientist came along by the name of Ptolemy who "solved" some of the problems with Aristotle's model. He proposed that the planets within the spheres were not directly

---

[11] J. D. Myers and Phil Newman, *Starchild Question of the Month for February 2013,* 2013.
http://starchild.gsfc.nasa.gov/docs/StarChild/questions/question54.html [Accessed April 1, 2015].

attached to the spheres, but to circles that were attached to the them. Even though the ancient world believed the universe to be enormous, they believed that the only planets in existence were those in our solar system.[12] They did not know about all of the planets that we know of today. Within this same model, the planets that were considered part of our galaxy were thought to have been the only planets in the universe. As time went on more planets were discovered inside of our solar system and then it was discovered that we are just one of many galaxies. Their minds would be absolutely blown to know what we know about the universe. It is no wonder that, when Copernicus and Galileo came along, the world had a hard time accepting what they had to say.

Sadly, by the time these two revolutionary figures arose, the Church had already adopted the ancient Greek model for the universe. It was in 1500 A. D. that Copernicus came on the scene and proposed a heliocentric model for the earth. This was after 2000 years of indoctrination of the geocentric model. Famously, Copernicus proposed that the earth was not the center of the universe and

---

[12] Astronomy 161 The Solar System, *The Universe of Aristotle and Ptolemy,*
http://csep10.phys.utk.edu/astr161/lect/retrograde/aristotle.html [April 1, 2015].

that he had conclusive evidence that could support his claim.[13] About a hundred years later Galileo took position of the thorn in the side of the Catholic Church and affirmed Copernicus' observation that the earth was not the center of the universe.[14]

It is troubling to many Christians to consider that the church has been horribly wrong in its conclusions about the universe. I will concede that there are challenging Biblical verses in this regard, but there are none that definitely state that the world is flat, that the earth is the center of the universe, or that the sun revolves around the earth. The Bible is factually correct when it directly addresses matters that we would classify as scientific. Most references to creation are not done so as a strict account but as poetry. For instance, the reference verse for this chapter is often used by Christians to confirm that the Bible tells us the universe is expanding. Is that what the intention for this Scripture is within its context? It could be, in a manner of speaking, but it seems that the main intention is to express the

---

[13] Eric Weisstein, *Copernicus, Nicholaus (1474-1543)*, 1996-2007.
http://scienceworld.wolfram.com/biography/Copernicus.html [Accessed April 1, 2015].

[14] *Galileo, 2015, The Biography.com website,* 2015, http://www.biography.com/people/galileo-9305220#death-and-legacy [Accessed April 2, 2015].

author's awe in the face of God's amazing power. Because it is not stated expressly in an account of creation or in a narrative style, we have to be careful with how we interpret this part of Scripture. This verse should not prevent us from concluding that the stretching is in reference to the expansion of the universe, but take caution in interpreting it in such a way.

It is commonly believed that the expansion of the universe is the result of the Big Bang. There are several difficulties with this theory. 1) Nobody knows if the Big Bang really happened. It is a little known fact that about every month or so a scientific study comes out that proves that the Big Bang did not happen. What typically happens is a day or so after the article is released another article talks about some of the science behind the Big Bang, pretending as though nothing has ever contradicted the idea. To me it appears that the so-called reality of the Big Bang depends on the day of the week more so than sound science. It should be considered pop-science, not real science. 2) Nobody knows if the universe is really expanding.

Based on observations it seems reasonable to suggest that the universe is expanding, but what do we truly know about our observations? Our observations used to suggest that everything revolves around earth. Later on we made better observations. Let me say that again. We made better observations, reinterpreted old observations, and created a model that more accurately represented reality. We should have learned our lesson not to look at the natural universe with narrow and dogmatic glasses. It *looked* like the planets revolved around us, but they did not. It looks like the universe is expanding, but is it? If the universe is expanding, is the Big Bang the only explanation? We need to be very careful with our conclusions. We live in an enormous universe and we really do not know a lot about it yet.

And 3) there are many inconsistencies in the universe that contradict the Big Bang model that warrant a new theory/model. The mainstream "scientific explanation" for these inconsistencies is to invoke mystical, magical, but absolutely natural, and material powers that cannot be seen and cannot be measured in any sort of way. Let me walk that back some. I am referring to *dark matter* and *dark energy* and I am not saying these forces do not exist. I am only scrutinizing these forces the same way secularists scrutinize the belief in God. Right now it seems like they invoke the possibility of these forces solely to save the Big Bang model.[15] If

---

[15] Nola Taylor Redd, *What is Dark Matter,* 2013. http://www.space.com/20930-dark-matter.html [Accessed March 31, 2015].

a creationist would resort to the argument "God did it" as an explanation for any phenomenon, he or she would be laughed at, and in most instances rightly so. The fact that secularists are able to commit the same intellectual crime, but invoke immeasurable and invisible "natural" explanations is clearly a double standard. I think they ought to be held to the same standard as creationists. Clearing the path for one's theory solely for the sake of a bias is not science and should be exposed as such a scandal.

One way or another there is not a single explanation for the expansion of the universe. One side of the debate sees the expansion of the universe and says "Big Bang." When the other side looks at the expansion of the universe they conclude that the universe had a definite starting point. As we observe the expansion of the universe we also observe the laws of physics playing out and the old adage from the Bible playing out in an incredible cosmic fashion: "There is nothing new under the sun."[16] As the universe expands we do not see a growing complexity to the system of the universe. Some people claim that new planets are forming, but thus far there has not been an observed birthing of a star. Even as the stars explode in magnificent supernovae, the first Law of Thermodynamics continues to operate while its brother the Second

[16] Ecclesiastes 1:9

Law dissipates its remains and distributes them into the vast nothingness of space. Either this system is just some sort of eternal celestial ballet or it had a starting point.

The logical conclusion according to common sense would be that the universe cannot be eternal, but that it had a starting point. In a popular manner of speaking most people that believe in the Big Bang and people that believe in God also believe that there was a definite starting point to the universe. The expansion of the universe implies that there was a time when it was not as expansive as it is in its current state. This naturally implies a starting point of some sort and a starting point implies causation. Is it possible that the universe could have begun without a cause? Let us say that all things are possible but some things are profoundly absurd and improbable. It is much more reasonable to suggest that there was some sort of cause to set the universe in motion and I would like to suggest to you that this cause had to have been supernatural based on the principles discussed in the chapters concerning the Laws of Thermodynamics.

THE ANTHROPIC PRINCIPLE

For this is what the LORD says –
he who created the heavens,
he is God; he who fashioned and made the earth,
he founded it;
he did not create it to be empty, but formed it to be inhabited –
he says:
"I am the LORD,
and there is no other."
~Isaiah 45:18

The Anthropic Principle is the idea that the universe appears as though it has been designed to house life. Most of this argument is based on the fine-tuning of the universe. If such and such factor was changed ever-so-slightly, life would be impossible in this universe. One of the fascinating aspects of this principal to me is that it is compelling enough to the mainstream scientific community that I actually read about the Anthropic Principle inside of my Physics textbook at Cleveland State University. This textbook states, "the Anthropic Principle, which says that if the universe were even a little different than it is, we could not be here. It might even seem that the universe is exquisitely tuned, almost as if to accommodate us."[17]

When it is said that the universe looks as though it was designed to harbor life, what is meant is that it is finely tuned in such a manner that if one of its variables were even slightly different, life would cease to exist. One of the physical variables that is taken the most for granted is gravity. Robin Collins describes the fine tuning of gravity with the imagery of a colossal dial that spans from one end of the universe to the other with one-inch increments. The dial represents all of the forces throughout the universe where gravity is the weakest force and the strong nuclear force is the strongest. Gravity could be as weak as it currently is or as strong as the most powerful force strength on this dial. If someone were to ask you to adjust the dial from where it currently stands and you decide to only move it one-inch you would bring devastation upon any life that might exist in the

---

[17] Douglas C. Giancoli, *Physics* (Upper Saddle River, New Jersey: Pearson Prentice Hall, 2005), 943.

universe. That one-inch adjustment would increase the force of gravity a billion-fold. Life, as we know it, would cease to exist.[18]

The cosmological constant, which is the energy density in empty space, is another finely tuned constant in the universe. Albert Einstein came up with the cosmological constant in 1917 to explain how the universe would not collapse on itself given all of the energy he thought it had in combination with the idea that the universe is unchanging. He later discarded the idea once he realized that the universe was expanding.[19] Today many scientists believe that the cosmological constant invented by Einstein is actually real and that it can be used to understand the existence of dark energy. So is it a real factor or not? It is hard to say, but there are certain factors in physics today that depend on it in order to prevent certain theories from falling apart. So for the time being we can assume that the cosmological constant or something of its sort is a reality for the sake of this illustration.[20] The

---

[18] Lee Strobel, *The Case for a Creator* (Grand Rapids, Michigan: Zondervan, 2004), 131-132.

[19] Carnegie Institution for Science, *1917: Albert Einstein Invents the Cosmological Constant.* https://cosmology.carnegiescience.edu/timeline/1917 [Accessed April 2, 2015].

cosmological constant is regarded by many physicists to be the greatest problem of all of physics. The likelihood of the cosmological constant randomly being tuned precisely to the degree that would allow life is like throwing a dart from light years away and hitting a bull's-eye on earth that is one trillionth of a trillionth of an inch. The likelihood of that happening are pretty much zero.[21]

Just these two factors alone aligning for life to emerge is highly unlikely. Now imagine the reality that there are even more forces in the known universe that are finely tuned along these lines that must also be set precisely so that life would be possible to exist in the universe. And this fine tuning is not just in the majesty of the cosmos, but it goes all the way down to the finest levels of life. Imagine that enormous dial spanning from one end of the universe to the other, once again, with one inch increments and now imagine that it is a combination lock. In order for the lock to accomplish the desired results you must blindly guess what twelve numbers on this lock will bring

---

[20] Clara Moskowitz, *Einstein's Biggest Blunder Turns Out to be Right,* 2010. http://www.space.com/9593-einstein-biggest-blunder-turns.html. [Accessed April 2, 2015].

[21] Strobel, 133-134.

about the desired results. Try to imagine guessing the twelve numbers needed to bring about life on this cosmic combination lock with billions upon billions upon billions of possible numbers. The likelihood of guessing the correct numbers at random would be virtually impossible.

Of course, part of the excitement of the Anthropic Principle is the possibility that other forms of life could emerge throughout the universe. This, of course, would happen through evolutionary processes. Lawrence Krauss, however, makes a very good point. Generally speaking, the universe, as a whole, has not been designed to support life.[22] So far, the only planet we have observed life on is earth. This would make the rest of the universe a rather marvelous burial place for what little life exists in comparison to its vastness. In suggesting this, I think that Krauss and even those who propose the Anthropic Principle are missing its entire point.

The universe is indeed designed to sustain life, but not on every planet. Only earth has been designed in such a way that life can exist. One could speculate that maybe other planets had been

[22] Lawrence Krauss, Intelligence squared: Think Twice, *Science Refutes God*, 2012. http://intelligencesquaredus.org/debates/past-debates/item/728-science-refutes-god [Accessed March 30, 2015].

prepared to sustain life if people moved away from earth. Life, however, cannot just happen spontaneously throughout the universe, let alone earth. Still, the thought that extraterrestrial life exists is fun. To hear that life does not exist on other planets is disappointing to some people. I have run this news by some of my friends and their reactions are always fun to receive. They will say things like, "How would you know?" "Why do you think that God would limit life to just earth?" "The universe is awfully big for there to only be life on earth." And "blah, blah blah, blah blah." Listen, the possibility of life on other planets sounds very exciting, but it is just not realistic.

There is no evidence that any sort of life has ever existed on any other planet aside from earth. When I say no evidence I mean zero, zilch, nada. Every now and then we have claims of people being abducted by aliens, seeing flying saucers, and other strange events. I, by the way, am not as quick to dismiss them as other people are, but there still remains no evidence, even if there is some authenticity to these claims. The evidence presented so far has not been compelling and is highly suspect. I have heard in movies that the reason that the evidence for extraterrestrials is not disclosed by the government is because we are not ready to know that we are not alone in this universe. What does that even mean? Does that mean that religious people are too stupid to accept the existence of extraterrestrials? If so, what would be the result of their lack of preparedness to receive such news? I do not see any real reason, that if there was evidence for extraterrestrials why it would be hidden from the general public.

On the other hand, it is very clear that earth is suitable for life. For one, it actually harbors life. This alone is proof of its sufficiency. Two, when the universe appears utterly void of life, earth has not only proven that it can sustain the life that exists today but that it once harbored far more life than what currently exists. With that in mind we can easily conclude that earth is a very special planet. But what determines whether or not a planet is suitable for life?

One of the first factors that is always looked at is, "Does the planet have water?" Whenever scientists discover water on a planet they become excited because the belief is that if there is water, there may be life.[23]

Second, although it probably should be first, is that the planet needs an atmosphere. The

[23] NASA, *Mars, Water, and Life.* http://mars.jpl.nasa.gov/msp98/why.html [Accessed April 2, 2015].

atmosphere separates the inner space of a planet with its outer space. This is significant because it protects life from the deadly vacuum of space. It also helps to regulate the temperature and overall climate of the planet. It keeps certain gases in and lets other gases out. It also protects life from the full danger of the sun's ultraviolet rays. The atmosphere is vitally important for life's existence.[24]

Third, is the planet a suitable temperature for life? If the earth were just a little farther away from the sun, it would be too cold to sustain life. If it were just a little closer to the sun, it would be too warm to sustain life. Life on planet earth has the advantage of not being too far away or too close. This definitely makes life more viable on earth.

There are other factors that are considered necessary for life, but there is a fatal flaw to the assumptions that meeting these criteria share: they all assume that evolution via abiogenesis happens and that it can happen anywhere in the universe. I personally do not take the idea that extraterrestrial life exists, in the form of aliens, seriously. Considering the clear teachings of the Bible it does

---

[24] *Hubble Site, Discovering Planets Beyond: Alien Atmospheres.*
http://hubblesite.org/hubble_discoveries/discovering_planets_beyond/alien-atmospheres [Accessed April 2, 2015].

not seem as though God created intelligent life outside of humans, unless you were to consider other spiritual beings like the angels. Even considering scientific investigation in the 21st century there is no evidence that would support the existence of extraterrestrial life. This may disappoint many people, but it is a simple reality.

Regardless, it is irrelevant as to whether or not the universe was fine-tuned for the sake of life. The only thing that matters is that the earth, with or without the help of the universe, is suitable for life. Factors within the universe make it possible for life to exist on earth and the majority of the scientific community will agree that a change in even one of these variables might be detrimental to life on earth. Life elsewhere in the universe has never been observed. If it were to be found it would open up the case for evolution, unless these lifeforms were to suggest that they too were created. So far it does not look like there are any other lifeforms in the universe, which makes the words of the Bible all the more important.

DNA

And even the very hairs of your head are all numbered. ~Matthew 10:30

The people in the world of Jesus did not understand how much God loved and cared about them, not to say that we know any better. In the passage above, Jesus used an illustration that even we today would struggle to comprehend. To think that God has numbered every hair upon our heads almost seems tedious and redundant for an all-powerful deity, but not for the God of the Bible. This illustrates that God knows how many hairs we have on our heads and that he intentionally designed each and every one of them. This is a level of intimacy between the Creator and the creation that should baffle us. With this illustration in mind, the world of Jesus did not know about DNA. If God designed each individual hair on each one of our heads, could we also assume that he paid as much attention to the construction of our DNA?

DNA is one of the most incredible discoveries inside of living organisms. The movie *Jurassic Park*, although fictional, gave a good description of DNA by referring to it as the blueprints for a living thing.[25] It is marvelous to look at and mind blowing to study. In examining how DNA proves creation, let us first examine what DNA is.

DNA is the shortened name for deoxyribonucleic acid. According to the Genetics Home Reference, DNA is hereditary material. It is found inside of every cell of an organism and is nearly identical in every single one. DNA is wrapped into a double helix formation and along its spine are four chemical bases, adenine, guanine, cytosine, and thymine. The sequence of these bases determines what information is necessary for upholding the structure of an organism.[26] Without DNA, the construction of proteins required for specific tasks would be impossible because they

---

[25] Michael Crichton, Steven Spielberg, *Jurassic Park* (Universal Pictures: 1993)

[26] Genetics Home Reference, *What is DNA?* 2015. http://ghr.nlm.nih.gov/handbook/basics/dna [Accessed April 2, 2015].

indeed contain the blueprints for all necessary proteins.

Tracing the construction of a protein might help us understand why DNA is important. The process starts when a polymerase produces a single strand copy of the DNA's original instructions. A messenger RNA is constructed inside of the polymerase as individual bases are positioned and added to the strand. The polymerase releases the messenger RNA which passes through the nuclear pore complex which recognizes information and controls the flow of information in and out of the cell's nucleus. The genetic assembly instructions of the messenger RNA passes through a ribosome which is the site of protein synthesis. Pausing here for a moment, notice that the RNA contains *instructions.* Instructions are a set of information that aids someone in building something. Inside of the ribosome, translation begins and a specifically sequenced chain of amino acids is built according to the instructions on the transcript. Now, not only do we have instructions but also *translation.* This means that some highly advanced processes are occurring inside of our cells. After the chain of amino acids is constructed, it is transported by transfer RNAs which link specific sequences of bases to corresponding amino acids which will ultimately determine what protein will be constructed. The amino acid chain is transported to a barrel shaped machine which folds it into the precise shape required to perform its function. Once it is folded into a protein it is ready to be used in the cell.[27] DNA provides the information to make this all possible.

It is unfortunate that the early architects of the theory of evolution were not aware of DNA. DNA is one of the most remarkable components of all living organisms. Built within DNA is a digital coding system. Software engineers look at DNA and recognize that it operates much like a piece of software. Bill Gates commented on the sophistication of DNA's information: "DNA is like a computer program but far, far more advanced than any software ever created."[28] Along the spine of DNA are four bases that function like alphabetical digital code. The four bases along the spine provide DNA with ability to make itself and to rebuild itself. Taking this into consideration, Gates is correct that DNA is more advanced than any software system.

---

[27] Stephen Meyer, *Signature in the Cell*. https://www.youtube.com/watch?v=TVkdQhNdzHU (HarperOne: New York, 2014) [Accessed March 31, 2015].

[28] Bill Gates, *The Good Road Ahead*. http://www.goodreads.com/quotes/336336-dna-is-like-a-computer-program-but-far-far-more [Accessed April 2, 2015].

One of the most famous experiments in the modern era was the Miller-Urey experiment. In 1953, Stanley Miller and Harold Urey conducted an experiment that attempted to explain the evolution of inanimate material into life. They constructed an environment with conditions that supposedly resembled a primitive atmosphere. When all was said and done, the experiment successfully yielded amino acids; the building blocks of proteins. Since proteins are one of the most important components of life, it was believed that their experiment was a success.[29]

Later on their research came under much scrutiny. The environment they created was deemed to be an inaccurate model of what the world would have been like at the emergence of life event. Even the results were not satisfactory. There was no evidence that amino acids, by themselves could be arranged into complex proteins. If the amino acids were arranged in the wrong order it would become a useless strand. Although their experiment was initially received with fanfare it only took about a decade before scientists began to denounce it in droves. The atmosphere was wrong and the model it was derived from was outdated. The chemicals that an *accurate* atmosphere would produce would be toxic. Ultimately even if amino acids could be

---

[29] *Biology*, 66

produced through such an experiment they would not have the information necessary for doing anything significant.[30]

With the DNA revolution of the 1950s more problems were discovered. It was discovered that DNA creates RNA, which communicates with ribosomes to create proteins. In order for amino acids to be sequenced properly messenger RNA must first exist. DNA has to be present in order for this to all work. If I were to fall into a pit and say that I will just go home and get a ladder to climb out, I would be using the same logic as an evolutionist when it comes to the emergence of life. If DNA is required in the process to communicate what proteins to create, how can protein come into existence without DNA first being present? The only way that an amino acid is useful is if an organism already exists that has DNA which can create RNA to communicate with the amino acids to form properly sequenced chains to form different sorts of proteins. The process of cell creation without a Creator becomes a chicken-or-the-egg problem. What came first, the amino acid or the cell? Logic would suggest the cell, but the evolutionist cannot believe such a premise if they want to have a secular starting point. In the 1970's,

---

[30] Strobel, 37-39

however, a new problem was discovered for those who believed in design.

Susumu Ohno published *Evolution by Gene Duplication* which proposed that a significant percentage of an organism's genome is composed of "junk." This *junk DNA* appeared to lack any significant functionality. In 1980, none other than the father of the DNA revolution stated, "Much DNA in higher organisms is little better than junk." (Francis Crick (1980) Nobel Laureate). In 1984 the Human Genome Project was launched. One of the major observations from this research was that a significant portion of the human genome was made up of *junk DNA*. In 2003, Jianzhi Zhang updated the classic research of Ohno. He wrote about pseudogenes, which are basically the equivalent to *junk DNA*,

> "Pseudogenization, the process by which a functional gene becomes a pseudogene, usually occurs in the first few million years after duplication if the duplicated gene is not under any selection. Nevertheless, some duplicated genes had been maintained in the genome for a long time for specific functions, before recently becoming pseudogenes because of the relaxation of functional constraints."[31]

His bias toward evolutionary processes is evident within this analyses because he could not have accomplished millions of years of research to prove his timetable for pseudogenization. Conclusions like this were typical in propagating the myth of *junk DNA*.[32,33]

These pseudogenes and *junk DNA* are assumed to be a vestige of the past. Because science is dominated by evolutionary ideologues, the observation that the majority of DNA was non-functional went unquestioned. It is in large part because of this belief in *junk DNA* that humans and apes are thought to share 98% of their genetic material.[34] Recently, it has been discovered that

---

[31] Jianzhi Zhang, Trends in Ecology and Evolution vol. 18, No6, *Evolution by Gene Duplication: An Update,* 2003. http://www.umich.edu/~zhanglab/publications/2003/Zhang_2003_TIG_18_292.pdf [Accessed April 2, 2015].

[32] Adam Siepel, Cold Spring Harbor, *Darwinian Alchemy,* 2015*: Human genes from noncoding DNA.* http://genome.cshlp.org/content/19/10/1693.full.html [Accessed April 2, 2015].

[33] Stephen S. Hall, Scientific American, *Hidden Treasures in Junk DNA,* 2012. http://www.scientificamerican.com/article/hidden-treasures-in-junk-dna/ [Accessed April 2, 2015].

[34] Dave Mosher, *Gorillas More Related to People Than*

junk DNA is not so junky after all. A certain portion of *junk DNA* is used to synthesize RNA. An increasing percentage of *junk DNA* is being found to be functional and as more is studied, and found to be functional, the larger the gap becomes between humans and apes. It has taken decades, between fifty and seventy five years, to finally acknowledge that these non-coding regions of DNA are functional. In this instance evolutionary biology held science back from advancing past this issue.[35]

Before uncovering the truth behind this myth, it was believed that 2% of DNA served any sort of function and that 98% was useless. The 2% that was deemed functional codes for proteins that our bodies need. The other 98% did not perform this function. The assumption was that DNA was uniform in its function and that it would only make sense that we have inherited useless DNA from our evolutionary ancestors. This evidence flew in the face of the faith community. Why would an all-knowing and all-powerful God need to program

Thought, Genome Says, 2012. http://news.nationalgeographic.com/news/2012/03/120306-gorilla-genome-apes-humans-evolution-science/ [Accessed March 31, 2015].

[35] Jeffery P. Tompkins, *RNA Editing: Biocomplexity hits a new high, 2015.* http://www.icr.org/article/8649 [Accessed April 2, 2015].

junk into his creation. The evolutionary community was quick to use this as evidence that we evolved through natural processes alone. It has been used in textbooks, classrooms, and debates to shame and confuse the opposition. Even though the evolutionary community now has thoughts on the non-junkiness of non-coding portions of DNA, theistic scientists have always had reason to believe that everything in our genetic code has an active purpose.

Creationist Dr. Georgia Purdom, who holds a PhD in Molecular Genetics, brings down the house in the *junk DNA* scandal. She cites research performed by a group known as ENCODE (Encyclopedia of DNA Elements) which specifically targeted a meager 1% of *junk DNA* inside of the human genome. They discovered functionality for 99% of the 1% that they studied. Functions that they either discovered or suspected were the ability to transcribe and translate DNA into proteins, performing valuable functions in transitioning DNA to RNA, a role in replicating DNA, and still some of which they are not yet certain. Nonetheless, the research they have done has made them enthusiastic about diving back into the genome to learn more about the functionality of this non-coding/*junk DNA*.[36]

---

[36] Dr. Georgia Purdom, *The Code of Life* (Answers in Genesis:

DNA is one of the most fascinating structures in the universe. Without it life would not be able to go on. Without life DNA would not exist. Evolutionary scientists attempted to highjack DNA for their own purposes but as research on DNA continues, it becomes more clear that DNA did not evolve naturally. Not only is DNA proof of a Creator, it is his personalized autograph on each and every living cell on earth.

St. Petersburg, Kentucky, 2007)

BIOLOGICAL PREDESTINATION

In him was life...~John 1:4

He is the image of the invisible God, the firstborn over all creation. For by him all things were created: things in heaven and on earth, visible and invisible, whether thrones or powers or rulers or authorities; all things were created by him and for him. ~Colossians 1:15-16

After having listened to the best arguments from both sides of the Creation/Intelligent Design vs. Evolution Debate, a new question arose. I have to admit that although I strongly disagreed with the notion that the universe is eternal, the argument is strong. In a scientific sense it is the only explanation that does not directly defy the First Law of Thermodynamics. In a philosophical sense, if it is nothing more than inanimate material and there is no God it makes a little bit of sense. But is it possible for an eternal universe, through its own laws and governing principles, to accidentally create life?

I considered everything I had heard and read about the universe's origins and it made me reflect upon the origins of life. Let us assume for a moment that the universe eternally fluctuates between a vast outer space and an infinitesimal point which is surrounded by basically nothing. In such a scenario laws of physics must exist to allow anything to happen at all. In this model it is clear that a vast universe is mandated through the laws of physics. If such a thing is true about the inanimate universe, what about life? Are there governing laws that mandate the evolution of life in the universe? It only makes sense that the answer would have to be yes.

Those who claim that random chance is responsible for the formation of life are either ill-informed or are lying to themselves. Think about it, nothing is truly random. Randomness does not really mean that something is unpredictable, just that something is seemingly unpredictable. If you are able to gather up enough data about any particular natural phenomenon you would be able to predict when it is about to occur. This is true even for the rolling of dice!

The mathematical odds of evolution from non-life to life are essentially zero to one. You would not take those odds with you to Vegas because you would be sure to walk away a loser. If life evolved without God there would have to be some sort of governing principle to mandate the evolution of life. It would change the odds life happening from zero to one, to one to one or 100%. In a material sense this would explain why life evolved. This would be a wonderful platform for investigating, materially, why life evolved.

"Why?" is a question that most atheists would rather avoid. Michael Shermer, the founding publisher of Skeptic magazine, an atheist, and Professor of Economics at Claremont Graduate University, is notorious for dismissing *why*. He claims that *why* is not important and *how* is all that matters. It sounds intelligent, but what is being avoided is a matter of genuine curiosity. *Why* is not just a sneaky way to invoke God, it is a genuine exploration of what other possibilities exist. In the case of the evolution of the first lifeforms, there must be some sort of underlying principle or physical law that mandates the emergence of life. If there is no principle, then there is no reason. If there is no reason, there is no *why*. If there is no *why*, there is no life, because there is no reason since there is no principle. Those that believe in God believe that he commanded the creation of life. Without God what in the universe would mandate the evolution of life?

Former atheist Dr. Dean Kenyon of San Francisco State University proposed a law to account for the materialistic emergence of life. When he reflected on the mystery of life's origin he knew that rationally something had to govern the creation of life. Despite his atheism he was able to recognize an order to the physical universe. After making considerable observations he wrote the book *Biochemical Predestination.*[37] In it he tried to explain the underlying principle that required the evolution of life. Not too long after he released his book, he was posed with many questions that challenged his theory. By nature, his argument was based on chemistry. It was a reasonable premise, but it did not play out well in the world of good science. After seeing that he could not answer these questions with intellectual honesty, he rejected his own proposal of biochemical predestination and accepted the fact that the origin of life requires a divine hand.[38]

[37] Dean H. Kenyon, *Biochemical Predestination*, (McGraw-Hill: New York, 1969).

[38] Written by W. Peter Allen and Stephen C. Meyer, Executive Producer James W. Adams, Director Lad Allen. *Unlocking the Mystery of Life,* (Illustra Media: La Mirada, California, 2010).

Let me propose a hypothesis that should be considered by both sides. I am calling it *biological predestination* as a nod to Dean Kenyon's *Biochemical Predestination.* Aside from chemical necessity, I am proposing the idea that life in the universe was not just random nor inevitable, but absolutely necessary. When the evidence is considered from either side, the one logical conclusion that should be made is that regardless of how it happened, life had to happen. In the Biblical sense, we cannot fully understand why God created life, but we do know that everything was created by him and for him. The creation of life was clearly a planned occurrence that God saw as necessary. What about the materialistic necessity for the emergence of life?

The unlikelihood of life teamed with our existence creates a huge dilemma for the atheistic community. Although secular scientists lay the burden of proof on creationists and Intelligent Design advocates, the burden of proof really falls on them. When nothing is content with being nothing and the inanimate has no reason to become animate why should anyone trust that life just accidentally happened? They also have to overcome the laws of nature including the theory of biogenesis.

Biogenesis is the observation that life can only come from life. A contradiction to this theory has never been observed which prompts certain people to call this the law of biogenesis. It is funny to think that the scientific community rejects spontaneous generation and accepts biogenesis. Spontaneous generation suggests that life can spontaneously arise from non-life. It used to be thought that flies grew out of rotting meat. This is laughed at today, but if you add millions of years to the equation, all of a sudden it is called sound science. To recap, science accepts biogenesis, which says that life can only come from life, rejects spontaneous generation, and says that Darwinian evolution just happened. Do you see the contradiction?

Abiogenesis is what the emergence of life from inanimate material is called. It has never been observed in nature and it has never been produced in a laboratory. The closest that science has produced inside of a laboratory experiment was the famous Miller-Urey experiment that produced amino acids, which is a far-cry from claiming that life emerged from non-life. Even the creation of the amino acids in the Miller-Urey experiment was hardly legitimate, but that is what gets taught in biology textbooks as proof for evolution. Life does not just spring up at random under any conditions.

Instead, some sort of governing principle must exist if Darwinian evolution were true.

There has to be some way for life to emerge from non-life because at some point life had to happen. If you follow the history of the evolutionary process it appears as though organisms today are not becoming any more sophisticated. The only significant changes that are observed today result from either a loss or scrambling of genetic information. If this principle is followed to its most logical conclusion, it would be reasonable to say that life existed before anything else. But that would sound too theistic.

If you are an atheist reading this book, I want to clue you in so that you might be able to develop a sound theory for the emergence of life. Dean Kenyon proposed biochemical predestination, which failed and he became a Christian. He ultimately saw that even though he was applying the sound rules of biochemistry nothing accounted for the information necessary for the formation of life. He scrapped his idea and no longer saw Darwinian evolution as a possible cause for life. His original hypothesis of biochemical predestination failed and brought him to God.

Where biochemical predestination says that life was inevitable, biological predestination suggests that life is a necessary part of the universe. This does not invoke God. In order for life to exist it must have occurred because the universe needed life to spring forth. The laws of physics forced the hand of the *blind watchmaker* and something marvelous happened. What would make life necessary? What forced the hand of progress? That is something for those who do not believe in God to ponder. If you are an atheist, notice that I am trying to help you out with your own theory. A useful illustration would be to think of the universe at its origin as a newborn baby.

Even though a baby is a complete human it is not a fully mature human. As a baby grows it develops the strength to lift its head. Why? Because it needs to lift its head in order to survive. A little later, the baby develops the ability to roll. Why? Because it needs to move if it wants to survive. One day the baby develops a lot of courage and decides to walk. This is monumental in a child's development because now he or she is able to be self-sufficient. The child learns to run and continues to grow bigger and bigger. Why does a child grow? If an adult human wants to take on the world it is an advantage to be bigger than a toddler. In an evolutionary sense, you are contending with savage beasts and you need every advantage you can get. After about twelve years, there is a stage of human development that changes the game for the rest of a person's life: Puberty. Hormones go crazy. Boys become strong and girls get prettier. Boys become attracted to girls and girls...well, they mess with boys' minds. Why? Because it ensures that in the future there will be offspring and that the offspring will be well-nurtured by the mother and well-protected by the father. This is just a chunk of human development, but why does all of this happen? Because if humanity wants to continue to exist they must go through a process of growth and maturity. If these stages did not happen you would never arrive at a fully grown and mature adult.

Think about the universe in a new way. Like everything else, it is a system. It is a much bigger system than any other that we can comprehend but maybe in order for it to exist everything else must exist. Once again, do not misunderstand. I am not suggesting that asteroids need to collide with planets, stars need to explode, or that atrocious things must happen. These things are no more necessary than a nine year old boy getting shot and killed by a stray bullet fired by warring gangs. Such a thing is tragic and unnecessary in the course of that child's natural development and everyone else's. For my theistic friends, I want to remind you that I am helping the atheists here to devise a viable theory for life. I know that God uses such tragedies for his purposes, so hold tight. What I am saying is that those asteroids had to exist for the sake of the universe. The planets had to exist for the sake of the universe. Life has to exist for the sake of the universe.

Life, however, necessarily had to exist. We know that life had to emerge from non-life in defiance of the laws of nature and of the physical universe. We are dirt from planet earth. Yes, dirt. Whether you believe in evolution or not our present form was inevitable. We are far too incredible even in the context of the known universe to be a random accident. Our bodies are products of the most sophisticated information processing system in the universe and our heads contain the greatest marvel in the entire universe. The existence of plants, animals, and mankind were no mistake. Atheist, this is your problem because all you have come up with so far is a zero probability of even the simplest organism's existence. You are going to have to go all in if you want to win this argument, but if you do, you will discover that you have lost.

Let me put everything together for you thus far. We have established that there are laws of physics that govern the operations of the known universe. To defy these laws would require, by definition, supernatural activity. Strike one. We have established that life cannot randomly emerge at a 0 to 1 ratio but that the odds must be 1 to 1. In other words, life must be a necessary part of the universe. Strike two. The only cause that can defy the physical laws must be supernatural. The universe cannot purposefully create anything. Purpose requires intentionality, intentionality requires thought, thought requires a mind, and a mind requires life. Something living created life. Might I suggest to you that there is a reason why we call the God of the Bible the Living God? Excuse me for interrupting your moment of revelation, but I feel like it is necessary to remind you that was strike three.

Is life a necessary part of the universe? It seems only natural to say that it is. Whatever necessary role life plays in the universe there is inherent significance to everything that exists, even the asteroids that scar the faces of planets. Once again, life did not arise out of a 0 to 1 likelihood. That is truly impossible no matter how much time elapses. Before closing this chapter I want to turn our main question, "Is life a necessary part of the universe?" on its head. Is the universe necessary for life? Maybe asking the question the right way will help all of you former atheists wrap your minds around this principle.

IRREDUCIBLE COMPLEXITY

I praise you because I am fearfully and wonderfully made; your works are wonderful, I know that full well. My frame was not hidden from you when I was made in the secret place. When I was woven together in the depths of the earth ~Psalm 139:13-14

When examining the evidence for a Creator, it is only a matter of time before you come across the concept of irreducible complexity. Irreducible complexity is one of those topics that cannot be avoided in science classrooms. Just like the Anthropic Principle, it exposes an undeniable reality that transcends religious bias. It is easily one of the most spoken about evidences for a Creator.

Irreducible complexity poses a great threat to Darwinian evolution. Something that is irreducibly complex is, "a single system composed of several well-matched, interacting parts that contribute to the basic function, wherein the removal of any one of the parts causes the system to effectively cease functioning."[39] The entire point of the concept of irreducible complexity is that certain systems could not evolve in a gradual manner according to the popular understanding of the theory of evolution. Although the serious proponents of evolution attempt to shove this concept aside, they cannot ignore its challenge.

The classic illustration of irreducible complexity, in layman's terms, is the mouse trap. This illustration is excellent because it demonstrates the principles of irreducible complexity on multiple levels. A mouse trap, although relatively simple, is a single system that is composed of multiple functioning parts. You have the platform, the spring, the catch, the hammer, and the holding bar. If you remove the platform, the other parts have nothing to be anchored to. Without the spring the latch, catch, and hammer would not function. If you remove just one part of the mouse trap it no longer functions in the way that it was intended.

Many evolutionists have made the mistake of saying that this concept is no challenge to evolution.

---

[39] Michael J. Seng, *Darwin's Black Box*, (Free Press: New York, 2006) 39.

Using the same illustration, they modify it to fit their purposes. The platform by itself might make a really good paper weight or door stop. The hammer might make a really good tie clip, and so forth. The argument from an evolutionary perspective is that the mouse trap does work effectively as a system of parts to achieve a common goal, but without one component or another, it does not follow that the other parts cease to exist.[40]

Frankly, this argument is a straw man. Those who invoke the idea of irreducible complexity are not claiming that the separate components cannot exist independently, but that the evolution of an entire system would require all of the necessary components to come together at the same time. The likelihood of this is slim to none. Out of what necessity does the platform of a mouse trap need the other components if it is viable as a door stop? Out of what necessity will a hammer, that makes a perfectly good tie clip, become one of the most important parts of a mouse trap? The logic is that, given millions of years of evolution, odds are that it

---

[40] Nat Johnson and Natural History Magazine (producers), National Center for Science Education, *Blind Evolution or Intelligent Design?*, The American Museum of Natural History: New York, April 23, 2002.
https://www.youtube.com/watch?v=CmMVgOTCukQ [Accessed March 31, 2015].

will happen. Instead of facing the reality, evolutionists choose the *anything is possible* approach. Using the same approach I should not be surprised if tomorrow the sky is saturated with flying pigs. If you deny that this is going to happen then you are denying the possibility and are therefore unscientific. You just need to use your imagination a little.[41]

In a purely mathematical sense the odds of the first evolutionary event happening were zero. For a moment, let us suspend the meaning behind the zero probability of the first evolutionary event and move to the second evolutionary event. What do you suppose the odds for the second evolutionary event would be? The probability of this was probably zero to one again. Consider all of the obstacles that the second evolutionary event, whatever it was, would have to overcome. The first evolutionary event would have required inorganic and inanimate material coming together to form a single cell organism. Fantastic. We still have a problem. After billions of years in the making there is a single cell organism. This single cell must learn how to survive the harsh environment in which it was born, eat so that it might remain alive, and then reproduce to ensure a future for its kind. I will grant the evolutionist as far as the first assertion that it must

[41] Behe, 43.

survive the harsh conditions based on their argument that it would have been adapted to survive under such extreme circumstances. But how did it instinctually know it needed food? Why would it crave anything? How did it reproduce? Was it asexual or sexual? I think we all assume it was asexual, but why and how did it choose to reproduce itself when it was not even aware of itself? I find it likely that if a single cell randomly evolved it probably would have had a very short lifespan. After billions of years in the making, the first organism dies and must start over from scratch, requiring billions years more to get it right. This is under the assumption that something is trying to emerge from the primordial goo. If life did not know it was supposed to arise from the goo, why would it have done so? The first event would have been like having a Royal Flush when your poker buddies have no money. It happened, but nothing resulted. Or like a tree falling in the woods with no one around to hear it. Did it actually make a noise? The difference is that we exist. This is evidence that life happened, we just do not know how. If we accept the premise of irreducible complexity we might come one step closer to the ultimate answer.

The classic biological example of irreducible complexity is spoken about in depth by Dr. Michael Behe. As a biochemist, Behe challenges the theory of evolution at a level that not many people can. It is in his book, *Darwin's Black Box*,[42] that he familiarizes his audience with a clear example of an irreducibly complex microorganism. This microorganism is known as the bacterial flagellar motor. Without going into great detail, this microorganism has parts that are described as *universal joints, propeller, drive shaft, and rotor.* If you were to see a picture of this biological machine, you would realize that these were not just cute names to describe parts that they resembled, the names of these parts *are* what they call them. If you were to walk into the middle of one of Behe's lectures on this topic, if you did not know where you were, you might suppose that he was talking about a car or an airplane. This bacterial flagellar motor is nothing short of a machine. Some of the parts to make this biological machine function at its peak performance are necessary in order for it to function at all. I could be generous and say that this does not necessarily rule out Darwinian evolution, but Behe, the biochemist, does rule it out as a viable process to explain this system.[43]

---

[42] Michael J. Behe, *Darwin's Black Box*, (Free Press: New York, 2006).

[43] Behe, 71.

When it comes to irreducible complexity we see examples mostly in the form of micro-organisms but some of the best evidence for irreducible complexity is found in much larger organisms. As we are all aware, evolution is all or nothing. If something goes wrong with an evolutionary adaptation and that particular creature dies as a result, that organism is now extinct and does not get a second chance. Creatures today have marvelous systems in place that defy the logic of evolution. Too often the mantra in biology classrooms is, "Wow, it is incredible that evolution created this." Instead of blindly accepting the evolutionary premise it is wise to examine the evidence for yourself. Take, for instance, the bombardier beetle.

The bombardier beetle is one of the most amazing creatures in the world. This tiny bug literally harbors explosive chemicals inside of its body. These chemicals are used as a defensive mechanism against anything that may seek to cause it harm. This in itself is incredible, but what prevents this beetle from blowing itself up? It actually has a couple of different chemicals that it uses. One of the chemicals stops the flammable chemical from getting out of control and killing the beetle. Question: What component of this process evolved first? Follow up question: Why?

What would the likelihood or necessity be for the bombardier beetle to evolve any one of these chemicals separately? It certainly could not have evolved the explosive element first, because without the other it would be deadly. The only reasonable alternative would be to say that it evolved the neutralizer first. Why would the beetle then evolve an explosive chemical and how would the beetle know how to wield it as a weapon? Too many questions plague an evolutionary explanation for this creature. It is easier to say that this beetle did not evolve, it had a Creator. Is it possible that God designed this creature in such a brilliant fashion that it would not harm itself? The woodpecker faces similar evolutionary problems.

You probably do not consider the woodpecker to be anything special, but consider what it does. We all know what a woodpecker does, it pecks at wood. Here is a challenge for you (do not do this): go outside, find the nearest tree that is considerably thick, and start slamming your head up against it as hard as you can. Are there any takers to this challenge? Maybe now you appreciate the woodpecker a little more. The woodpecker does this routinely in order to find food.

Its anatomy is adapted in such a way that it can chip away at a tree with its beak and remain virtually unharmed. First of all, its feet are designed differently from most birds so that it can latch onto a tree and maintain a vertical posture. To aid its stability it has specially designed tail feathers that are more firm. This allows the woodpecker to brace itself in a tripod position using its feet and tail feathers. Clearly, its beak is more durable than most birds' and it strikes the tree with incredible precision. To absorb the shock from striking the tree, it has a special layer of cartilage between its beak and its skull. This cartilage prevents the woodpecker from killing itself. In order to reach inside of the tree, it has a tongue that projects ten inches past its beak. This is incredible, but not enough for it to catch a good meal. In order for it to catch its prey, it has barbs at the end of its tongue and a special glue-like adhesive. Whatever it barbs becomes stuck to its tongue. When it catches its prey and pulls it into its mouth, it produces a special solvent to dissolve the glue. If it did not dissolve the glue, it would swallow its tongue and probably choke to death. How could the woodpecker evolve slowly and progressively without going extinct? The evolution of such a creature does not make sense.[44]

There are many other examples of irreducible complexity. Without some sort of supernatural

---

[44] *David Hames, Incredible Creatures that Defy Evolution, vol. 1.* Exploration Films, Reel Productions, 2006.

guidance evolution could not produce systems like the ones discussed. Thus far, irreducible complexity has proven to be convincing and those who espouse its premise claim that as time goes on the evidence for it only becomes stronger. Without a doubt this is an irrefutable proof of creation.

NATURAL SELECTION

"Let the land produce living creatures according to their kinds: livestock, creatures that move along ground, and wild animals, each according to its kind." And it was so. ~Genesis 1:24

From the chapter title, you are probably wondering, does natural selection prove creation? You may be a little confused at this proposition but natural selection does seem to be a scientifically verifiable phenomenon that does help to confirm certain truths expressed in the Bible. The problem is that most people associate natural selection with Charles Darwin's theory of evolution. It is true that he popularized the mechanism of natural selection, but it is not necessary to assume that natural selection proves evolution or that it disproves God. In fact, I believe that with the level of research that has gone into proving natural selection, macro-evolution has actually been disproven.

In order to present natural selection in its truest form, a form that actually supports creation, one must first understand natural selection for what it really is. The way that most people learn about natural selection is in the context that it proves macro-evolution. It normally starts off as a story that explains how the world of science was once dominated by religious minds and was full of absurd theories, like the fixity of species and a flat earth, until Charles Darwin came and saved the day. Darwin's theory went on to liberate scientific minds from the bonds of superstition and eliminated the need for anybody to ever believe in God again. This is not quite the whole truth.

The story of Darwin is a little bit more sophisticated than what we are told in science books. He was highly influenced by minds that did not accept a proposed theory of a global flood. While sailing on the Beagle, Darwin read Charles Lyle's *Principles of Geology*[45] which proposed a geological model that required millions of years instead of catastrophism. A less popular book that Darwin had also read was Patrick Matthew's *Naval Timber and Arboriculture*,[46] which made reference to "This natural process of selection." Combining

---

[45] Charles Lyell, *Principles of Geology,* (Penguin Books: New York, 1997).

the ideas of an old earth geology, as proposed by Lyell, and a natural process of selection, proposed by Matthews, gave him the foundation for the theory of evolution.[47] So Darwin built his theory upon the backs of existing theories, of which he was already aware. This is far different from what is commonly taught. What is also neglected is that Darwin predicted what would need to be observed to falsify his thesis "the origin of species." He knew that his theory was incomplete and therefore could be disproved by future discoveries. One of the problems in Darwin's day was that not much was known about genetics or cells. Natural selection was a very observable phenomenon, but it would be decades before people could start understanding its limits.

Although it is a powerful force, natural selection has some very definite limits. One of its greatest limits would be that it only operates with organisms already in existence. Natural selection was never meant to be a theory to explain the

---

[46] Patrick Matthew, *Naval Timber and Arboriculture* (Neil & Co. Printers: Edinburgh, 1831)

[47] Ian Taylor, *In the Minds of Men: Darwin and the New World Order, fifth edition,* (TFE Publishing: Zimmerman, Minnesota, 2003)
http://www.creationism.org/books/TaylorInMindsMen/TaylorIMMe05.htm [Accessed March 31, 2015].

emergence of all life on earth. He never observed life evolving from non-life. Darwin's early observations were limited to that which was already living.

What he observed among the different lifeforms that he studied was a *phenotypical* change, not a change in *genotype*. The genotype is the genetic body of information. A phenotype is the expressed genetic characteristics. A change in the phenotype will definitely make an outward difference, but the genotype remains the same. Within all of the organisms that he observed, he never observed a change in the genetic information of any of them. Taking this concept to the laboratory helps confirm the limits of natural selection.

In 2010 an experiment was undertaken that observed 600 generations of fruit flies. The whole purpose of this experiment was to observe how advantageous mutations could become fixed within a population. The change they observed was nothing genetically new. It did not provide a significant advantage within the population of fruit flies. Perhaps an even bigger problem was that the change observed was not even "fixed" as the scientists conducting the experiment would have liked. The change observed was the ability to hatch earlier. In the grand scheme of things this is not a change that could be extrapolated into macro-evolution. It happened to be advantageous within the confines of the environment the fruit flies lived in, but as soon as conditions changed, the adaptation was lost. Although the results of this experiment speak for themselves, evolutionary scientists remained hopeful that these changes could pave the way for greater evolutionary events. Such a conclusion is illogical and it should be acknowledged that nothing significant happened in this experiment.[48] Experiments of this sort always yield these sorts of results. But evolutionists cling to their faith and believe in the unforeseeable. Their faith is not rooted in experimental data, but in something greater than the scientific method itself.

The faith of an evolutionist is profound in that it is rooted in the pseudoscience of Charles Darwin. If you study Darwin long enough you will notice that his theory was based on his observations of micro-evolution, homology, and geology. The reason why Darwin's science was pseudoscience was because it did not incorporate experimentation, strictly observations of the natural world. There is nothing necessarily wrong or disingenuous about this practice, but it is an argument commonly used

---

[48] *Fruit Flies and Advantageous Mutations,* 2010, https://answersingenesis.org/genetics/mutations/fruit-flies-advantageous-mutations/ [Accessed March 31, 2015].

against the community of faith. I also state this because there was a lot that Darwin did not know. Another limit on Darwin's research was the fact that he and other scientists assumed that cells were not complex. In the 21st century we realize that cells are more complex than our best technology. His initial observations were nothing more than observations, but they were made with a great sampling of creatures.

Even though Darwin himself was not particularly impressed with the finches he collected, it is one of the most popular illustrations of his evolutionary studies. He collected many finches as he travelled from island to island on his voyage and he began to notice the differences among his samples. It had appeared as though the finches were modified according to the demands of their environments. The differences from sample to sample were clear, but the similarities linked them all together. From this observation he was able to deduce that all of the finches descended from a common ancestor. This same phenomenon was present in other forms of life, as well. This made Darwin very curious. What was more staggering was the fact that similarities were not just observed from species to species, but even amongst totally different kinds of animals. This realization resulted in his most profound claim: all of life descended from a common ancestor.[49]

Darwin's theory became popular and other people started to notice the characteristics that many creatures share in common. The study of these similarities became known as homology. The most famous depiction of homology is a comparative picture showing the bone structure of a human hand, a bat wing, a horse leg, and a whale's fin in which it is shown that they all share an identical anatomical arrangement. The most infamous example of homology, as evidence for evolution, would be that of humans and other primates. Would it sound far-fetched to conclude that humans, chimps, and apes had a common ancestor? Primates are relatively smart, share similar behavioral habits, and are anatomically similar to humans. This leap of faith does not take much imagination. These observations alone, however, cannot infer that evolution took place.

Evolutionists must look to the past to find a history of evolution among the fossils of the geological column. Tracing it downward into the

---

[49] Truth in Science, *Darwin's Finches,* 2013. http://www.truthinscience.org.uk/tis2/index.php/evidence-for-evolution-mainmenu-65/53-darwins-finches.html [April 2, 2015].

earth, and backward in time, there is an interesting progression of simple to more complex organisms. More people are converted to evolution through fossil evidence than laboratory data. One of the most cited examples of fossil evolution is that of whales.

Whale evolution is often spoken of with absolute certainty. The supposed fossil trail starts off with a land mammal that resembles a cat known as sinonyx. Next we have a mammalian creature that spent lots of time in the water, ambulocetus. Rodhocetus, a mammal, which displays anatomy slightly more adapted for water life, is the next step in the evolutionary ladder. Then we have a creature called Dorudon which is essentially a whale with teeth. One of the later creatures in the chain is basilosaurus, which is an enormous marine mammal that was falsely given a reptilian name. The example of whale evolution, although frequently touted, has many problems.

The problems with whale evolution are well documented. Ambulocetus appears in higher strata than those of which fully formed whales first appear. This automatically eliminates the possibility that ambulocetus could have been an ancestor to modern whales. With rodhocetus, many assumptions about its anatomy were nothing more than hopeful guesses. The most notorious of which would be its fluked tail. No evidence of a fluked tail existed, but because it was believed that rodhocetus was a missing link, artistic depictions included it as an assumption. Not a single piece of evidence supported the evolutionary claim. This small sampling should be proof enough that small and progressive changes are not enough to account for whale evolution.[50,51]

Some would argue that apes alone are proof of human evolution. Is there a basis for such a claim? Yes and no. Genetically the two creatures share more in common than they do with other organisms, despite the widening gap being discovered in their genomes. One might suppose that the two shared a common ancestor, but to ignore their differences would be a mistake. The most obvious difference between other primates and humans is brain power. A human toddler has more brain power than an adult primate of any other species. Physically, humans and apes have entirely different feet, mouths, forelimbs, and hind limbs. We could proceed to argue on the basis of habits, genetics,

[50] Angela Meyer, *The World of Whales,* 1996. https://answersingenesis.org/aquatic-animals/the-world-of-whales/ [Accessed April 1, 2015].

[51] Dr. Carl Warner, *Evolution: The Grand Experiment,* 2014, http://www.thegrandexperiment.com/whale-evolution.html [Accessed April 1, 2015].

and so forth, but the biggest differences are intangible. Humans and animals are separated by far more than evolution can explain. The president of the Institute for Creation Research, Dr. John Morris, wrote,

> Creationists contend that while humans and apes have much in common (after all, we live in the same world, breathe the same air, eat the same kinds of food, have hearts that pump blood, etc.), the differences lie in other areas. Created in the image of God, mankind possesses the ability to communicate abstract thought, appreciate beauty, express love, and know right from wrong. Most importantly, man has an eternal spirit and can choose to accept or reject the Creator's kingship over their lives.[52]

Apes do not have the capability within their own cerebral limits to accomplish the differences listed by Dr. Morris. Could it be that Darwin was wrong with his initial conclusions? Was he observing evolution or was there something else that could account for his observations?

---

[52] John D. Morris, Ph.D. 1995. What Distinguishes Man From Ape?. Acts & Facts. 24 (11). http://www.icr.org/article/what-distinguishes-man-from-ape [Accessed April 1, 2015].

What Darwin observed is called micro-evolution. His finches were adapted to their respective environments. Their beak sizes varied, but were limited by their genetics.[53] Micro-evolution is not a change in the truest sense, but is due to natural selection and is based upon what trait is advantageous for an environment. The trait already exists within its genetic limits, but becomes a prevalent trait within a population because of an advantage that it provides. This is natural selection at work. It is demonstrably a legitimate process, but is better understood within the framework of the Bible.

Natural selection is an underlying principle of Biblical truth that can be read about in the book of Genesis. In its first chapter, after God created plants, fish, birds, land animals, and humans, he commanded them to be fruitful, multiply, and to bring forth after their own kinds. In a very real way God established the order of the natural world.

Creationists believe that the most significant division in the animal kingdom is what is referred to as the *kind.* In mainstream science, this term is

---

[53] Evolution News and Views, *Darwin's Finches Show Rule-Constrained Variation in Beak Size,* 2010. http://www.evolutionnews.org/2014/06/darwins_finches086581.html) [April 2, 2015].

nearly synonymous with what is known as the *family* categorization.

The Lord commanded that all living things should bring forth after their own family. Is this what is observed in the natural world today? This principle is so prevalent that we have never seen anything occur outside of the order that every living thing should bring forth after its own family. Although there is no solid definition for a *kind/family*, many have agreed that it is a group of animals that can reproduce with one another. In relation to a *species*, a family would be *dog* and the species would be *Chihuahua*.

Looking at dogs, it is clear that from species to species there are many differences. There are big dogs, small dogs, calm dogs, and energetic dogs. Some dogs are good at herding, some are good at hunting. Some dogs are only bred for luxury's sake. Regardless of what form or demeanor it takes, a dog is a dog. Generally speaking dogs can reproduce with other dogs even if they are not of the same species. Dogs can also reproduce with their wild cousins, wolves. No matter how many times a dog has been reproduced and no matter how odd of a variant might be discovered through selective breeding techniques, the offspring of two dogs will inevitably be more dogs. This is consistent with the Bible's teachings. The same thing has been observed among big cats, like lions and tigers, and among horse-like creatures, such as horses, zebras, and donkeys. Has there ever been an observed example of one kind or family of creature evolving into another?

This alternative has never been observed. A dog has never given birth to a cat, an ape has never produced a human, and you will never see a crocodile lay chicken eggs. Likewise, a dog cannot successfully reproduce with a cat, and so forth. There are not many, if any, principles in biology as evident as this simple point.

Natural selection is a very common sense process by which a kind of animal is able to adapt and survive under new ecological challenges. Sickle cell anemia is a characteristic that has become prevalent in Africa through natural selection. In Africa, malaria runs rampant and has killed many people. People that have sickle cell anemia cannot catch malaria which has resulted in a significant portion of Africa's population having this disease. In a normal population sickle cell is detrimental, even deadly. Nonetheless, it shows how natural selection enables a population to adapt in such a way to overcome challenges.

Natural selection was programmed by God for the survival of the different kinds of animals. After the Curse struck the world, life became susceptible to all sorts of evil. Many people wonder why God allows death and suffering and why he created predatory animals to prey on others. Both the predator and the prey have been prepared in advance to be able to survive in oppressive environments. Those who are the most fit for an environment, or a specific circumstance, will naturally survive, while the unfortunate unfit will inevitably die off, making way for nature's champions to thrive.

PROOF OF THE FLOOD

So the LORD said, "I will wipe mankind, whom I have created, from the face of the earth – men and animals, and creatures that move along the ground, and birds of the air – for I am grieved that I have made them." ~Genesis 6:7

One of the biggest events in the entire creation story found in Genesis is the worldwide flood. Today more and more Bible scholars have been renouncing their belief in the flood that occurred in the days of Noah. They believe that there is no physical evidence of a worldwide flood. Most of these scholars have instead adopted a creative interpretation of this flood event. They choose not to deny the existence of Noah, an ark, or even a catastrophic flood, but to redefine what the Bible says.

These scholars have chosen to define the worldwide flood as a local flood. They claim that the reason it was considered worldwide was because it flooded their entire *known* world at the time. They have reconstructed this flood from the Babylonian story, *Enuma Elish.* The assumption is that *Enuma Elish* might have been the first flood story. It has also been discovered that there is geological evidence that coincides with a massive flood event in the region of Mesopotamia.

To me, it is troubling that some of the greatest Bible scholars have conceded to a local flood. Understandably, they side with what they consider to be *the evidence*, but they allow non-believing sources to interpret the evidence for them. What is more troubling is that it appears as though they take the authority of a Babylonian myth over the authority of the Word of God concerning the flood event. I am not sure as to why, but they refuse to see the overwhelming evidence for a global flood. In the one instance this makes no sense to me, but then again they allow non-believing scientists that are supposedly experts in this field to interpret the data for them.

If we are to see the evidence of the flood, we must first understand what would have caused it to happen in the days of Noah. Without a doubt the Bible implies that it was a judgment against mankind and was by virtue supernaturally caused. Taking that into account it did not necessarily have to leave behind any evidence. But, since this event clearly took place in the physical world it should very well be expected that some sort of evidence would support its occurrence. There are many false assumptions but one of which seems to win the day in most discussions. This assumption is that all of the flood water came from rain. In the Genesis account, rain fell for forty days and forty nights. Most people assume that this massive amount of downpour was solely responsible for the flood. If we consider everything that the Genesis account says, we must also recognize that it describes in no uncertain terms that much of the water for the flood came from within the earth. This suggests that seismic activity was largely responsible for the flooding in the days of Noah.

The National Oceanic and Atmospheric Administration define a tsunami as "a series of ocean waves generated by sudden displacements in the sea floor, landslides, or volcanic activity. In the deep ocean."[54] It is recorded in Genesis that "all the springs of the great deep burst forth."[55] The Bible

---

[54] National Oceanic and Atmospheric Association, http://www.tsunami.noaa.gov/ [Accessed April 1, 2015].

[55] Genesis 7:11

acknowledges that the physical components of the flood water came from both rain and massive seismic activity. The description of the springs bursting is catastrophic imagery that probably implies earthquakes and volcanic eruptions that shook the foundations of the earth. Many creationists believe that the fault lines that separate the tectonic plates were created during this event. There is much evidence left behind that suggests a global flood if we are willing to open our eyes.

There are incredible geologic implications for the flood and unfortunately I will only be detailing one of the lines of evidence in this regard in this book. There is much evidence within the rocks of the earth that there had to have been a catastrophic flood event and this evidence is very convincing within itself. For now, the evidence that will be examined is concerning the effects that the flood had on life. In other words, when the Bible says that the flood wiped out all of the life on earth, geologically there should be evidence that the flood wiped out all of the life on earth. This would be preserved in the form of fossils. We will focus our attention on the so-called fossil record left behind as a result of the flood.

Fossils are a great testimony to the catastrophic nature of the worldwide flood. Evolutionists view fossils as evidence that the world is billions of years old and that the fossils themselves represent hundreds of millions of years of life's evolution. The popular understanding of fossils and geology is rooted in evolution. While you read the rest of this chapter, suspend what you think you know about fossils and consider the possibility that what you have been taught in school could be wrong.

Fossilization is not a simple process. Most living organisms today will not fossilize and most organisms of the past have not fossilized because certain things must happen in order for a fossil to form. In order to preserve the general form of a creature, it must be rapidly covered and pressed into the mud, ash, or whatever it was that enshrouded the formerly living thing. If this does not happen the creature will not likely become a fossil. The process of decay starts immediately after the body stops functioning. The body of a land animal does not last long after it dies. A sea creature does not fare any better and probably in most cases has less time to fossilize because of the ravages of an all water environment in combination with scavengers.

A strange phenomenon that defies the evolutionary model is fossilized sea creatures appearing in mountains. How do sea creatures appear in the mountains? As creationists are aware, the flood covered even the tallest mountains. The Bible speaks of how the flood was even responsible for forming some of the mountains that exist today. To avoid the accusation of circular reasoning, I will clarify. There were mountains before the flood, but today there are both new mountains and old mountains. The old ones are probably different than they were before the flood, while the new ones were created by the catastrophic events of the flood. Not much of a deal is made out of this in the mainstream, but mountains are actually somewhat of a mystery. Nobody truly knows where mountains came from in an evolutionary sense. Mainstream geologists have their theories concerning the formation of mountains.[56]

It seems as though the most accepted scientific theory on this topic deals with plate tectonics. The earth is divided up on tectonic plates separated by fault lines. These plates move and collide with one another, hence seismic activity which is often manifested in earthquakes. The force between these tectonic plates is theorized to cause a folding of the land mass, in a sense, and this between tectonic plates colliding in combination with underwater volcanic activity is thought to produce mountains over the course of millions of years. Even though

---

[56] Andrew Snelling, *Chapter 29: What Are Some of the Best Flood Evidences?* 2015. https://answersingenesis.org/the-flood/what-are-some-of-the-best-flood-evidences/ [Accessed April 2, 2015].

evolutionists have an exaggerated time frame, it is still interesting to see that they believe, as Genesis teaches, that the land rose out of the water in earth's formational stages. The popular understanding of mountain formation could be plausible if it were not for fossilized sea creatures within the mountains that exist above sea level.[57]

Where does the popular scientific model say these fossils in the mountains came from? The best explanation they have is that creatures were buried on the ocean floor in a place where a mountain was going to form and fossilized carcasses were elevated out of the water, over time, and were eventually elevated so high above sea level that they exist on top of what we call the mountains. The only problem with this theory is that there are tons of problems with this theory.

As earlier discussed, fossilization is a very delicate process in a very violent way. For sea creatures this is particularly difficult for reasons previously discussed but also because plate tectonics, the shifting sands of the ocean floor, and so forth. It would be amazing if a creature fossilized

[57] Schlumberger Excellence in Education Development, *The Earth – A Living Planet: Plates Borders & Mountain-Building, Building*, 2015.
http://www.planetseed.com/relatedarticle/plate-borders-mountain-building [Accessed April 1, 2015].

after having endured the ravages of the ocean. There are way too many fossils of sea creatures for us to say that they all formed as a result of slow processes. Is there a better explanation? The creationist model is far simpler, far more rational, and approaches the problem according to science in which we can be certain of.

These fossils are on top of mountains because they were buried rapidly in a global catastrophe and many of the mountains are the remains of that catastrophe. The evidence exists and it is a reasonable conclusion. However, the implications of a global catastrophic flood would shake the foundations of the discipline of science. As the great flood did to the world, so would the acknowledgment of the great flood cleanse the scientific community of corrupt theories and only leave the sound theories as a remnant. Ironically, within the past few decades, mainstream science has started to accept the reality of a global catastrophic event. They have not conceded that it was a flood, but they can no longer deny that a global catastrophe was a reality.

A grand mystery has infiltrated the realm of mainstream science. This mystery is a disappearing act which science has been trying to figure out for over 150 years. The scientific community has determined that unravelling this mystery and would provide a major clue for piecing together our evolutionary past. What is even more daunting is the reality that solving this mystery could save mankind from certain obliteration. If the most dominant creatures ever to walk the earth could be eliminated in what appears to be an overnight sort of purge, what can humanity expect in its future? Namely, this mystery is the extinction of the dinosaurs.

Dinosaurs were the pinnacle of the evolutionary world before the rise of technology. After millions upon millions of years of worldwide dominance, the dinosaurs all of a sudden disappeared. Years have been spent trying to find a gradual, uniformitarian, explanation to their disappearance. Having come up short, the scientific community had to venture outside of their comfort box. Catastrophism used to only be for creationists, but no other explanation could account for the sudden disappearance of dinosaurs.

65 Million years ago, the night sky blazed with light. A monolith of death sped toward the earth, striking her surface and unleashing a force comparable to the world's nuclear arsenal. The age of dinosaurs was over. Commemorating their doom is a massive crater off of the coast of the Gulf of Mexico. We call it the Chicxulub Crater.

The hypothesis is that the Chicxulub Crater was created by a massive asteroid that struck the earth. In fact, because of the evidence, we are fairly certain that such an event happened. Supposedly, when this asteroid struck the earth it brought the makings of death along with it. A massive explosion, toxic chemicals, dust that blocked out the sun, and possible tidal waves contributed to the death of whatever roamed the earth. The problem, however, is fairly suspicious. If there was a disaster that wiped out all of the dinosaurs around the world, how did anything survive?[58]

Ancient history might provide an answer to how there could have been a worldwide catastrophe that had the potential to kill all things, but failed to do so. This ancient model explains what happened to the dinosaurs and why life has continued on earth. The answer is so insultingly simple that science cannot accept it. It is a catastrophe that has been spoken of by just about every foreign culture. A flood so destructive that it wiped out all of life on earth, reshaped its landscape, and left a portfolio of death like none other. Unlike its opposing model, this model has a means of salvation called an Ark. It

---

[58] Charles Q. Choi, *Asteroid Impact That Killed the Dinosaurs: New Evidence,* 2015. http://www.livescience.com/26933-chicxulub-cosmic-impact-dinosaurs.html [Accessed April 1, 2015].

is said that the Ark preserved a small percentage of the world's population. This would explain how life was able to continue after a global catastrophe. What it does not explain is how the dinosaurs became extinct. Regardless, it lays a foundation for understanding their survival and how they eventually became extinct. This is as far as we will go with this topic for now because we have already established the likelihood of a global catastrophe that was responsible for widespread death. Aside from the dinosaurs, there is still much fossil evidence that needs to be considered in relation to our topic. If fossils are proof for creation why do most scientists disagree?

Prevalent within the discussion of how to interpret fossilized sea creatures above sea level is the reality that there is more than one way to interpret geological evidence. Realistically people can choose to believe either interpretation. Both follow a stream of logic, both have problems, and neither have living witnesses. How do you determine which of the two perspectives is more credible? The one that makes the best sense out of the facts without overcomplicating things should be considered the more likely of the two perspectives. As an example, let us examine the next geological reality, the Cambrian Explosion.

The Cambrian explosion is a geological period in time when the first life forms supposedly appeared. To clarify, this is more popular as an Intelligent Design argument than it is for a creationist. I disagree with the Intelligent Design interpretation but they do effectively throw a wrench into the accepted evolutionary model of life's creation. Geologically, before the Cambrian era there were no life forms. During the Cambrian era, there seemed to be an explosion of highly complex lifeforms. This might not sound like a big deal, but to secular evolutionists it is a big problem.

Tracing the theory of evolution back to life's origins, it is assumed that the first organism would have been a simple creature, like a single-celled organism, and from this simple creature would blossom all of the creatures that we know of today. One of the famous icons of evolution is the evolutionary tree of life that shows how all things descended from a common ancestor. In this model, the root is singular and the branches are many. In the Cambrian Explosion, the roots are many and the branches are many. What gives?

Following evolutionary logic, it seems as though complex life suddenly appeared spontaneously. Instead of simple creatures slowly evolving over long spans of time the fossil record shows that complex lifeforms appeared rapidly at the advent of life. This makes the likelihood of Darwinian Evolution not good. In fact, I would say that the Cambrian Explosion more or less disproves the evolutionary origin of life as we know it today.[59]

Considering creationism, how might one interpret the Cambrian Explosion? There is not much for a creationist to say. The Cambrian Explosion is neither a surprise nor an anomaly. If there was a catastrophic global flood, what is seen in the Cambrian strata would be expected. To be specific about the lifeforms found in the Cambrian strata, they are deep sea organisms. In the event of a global flood where the gates of the deep are opened up, a creationist would expect to see deep sea creatures buried in the deepest strata. To me this gives creationism a better explanation of the facts because we do not need an *explanation* concerning what we see because what we see is already consistent with what we believe.[60]

---

[59] Casey Luskin, *Erwin and Valentine's The Cambrian Explosion Affirms Major Points in Darwin's Doubt: The Cambrian Enigma is Unresolved,* 2013.
http://www.evolutionnews.org/2013/06/erwin_valentine_cambrian_explosion073671.html [Accessed April 1, 2015].

[60] Elizabeth Mitchell, *Cambrian Explosion or Creation Week – Key to Vertebrate Success,* 2015.
https://answersingenesis.org/theory-of-evolution/evolution-timeline/cambrian-explosion-or-creation-week-key-to-

After considering all of the death found within the depths of geology and noticing that much of the life represented in the geological column is extinct, one must wonder how creationists deal with the abundance of extinct lifeforms. Truth be told, there is no mystery to extinction. Whenever a population of creatures is reduced significantly it faces the threat of extinction under natural circumstances. Within the course of American history, another mechanism for extinction was exposed, namely, mankind. We have heard the stories of how the Native Americans depended on bison for their survival and would use bison for food, clothing, shelter, and other things. As America became more colonized and conflict increased between the natives and the settlers, the settlers decided to wipe-out all of the bison. Doing this caused much trouble for the natives and made overcoming them easier.[61]

Although most of the creatures found in the geologic column are extinct, there have been some surprises. We call these surprises *living fossils.* Living fossils, as I implied, are creatures found in the fossil record that are found alive today. Some of vertebrate-success/ [Accessed April 1, 2015].

[61]Globe Urban Internet Solutions, Bisonbasics.com, *A Brief History of Bison,*
http://www.bisonbasics.com/history/past_future.html [Accessed April 1, 2015].

these creatures were once thought to be extinct, while we have been aware of others for quite some time. A good example of a living fossil is the coelacanth. The coelacanth is a fish that, for one, was thought to be extinct, and, two, thought to be a transitional creature between fish and amphibians.[62] Not every living fossil is a creature that we once presumed extinct. We have actually never questioned the survival of most living fossils. Some of which that we are most familiar with are aardvarks, tuataras, nautiluses, platypuses, koalas, horseshoe crabs, and crocodiles. The amazing thing about all of the living fossils mentioned is that all of them exist in the same form as their fossils appear. This means that either they have escaped the power of evolution for hundreds of millions of years or that maybe there is a better explanation for their existence.[63]

Thus far we have considered a good sampling of the fossil evidence. We have looked at deep sea creatures imbedded in mountains, the extinction of

---

[62] Institute for Creation Research, *Living Fossils Display No Evidence of Evolution's Long Ages,* http://www.icr.org/living-fossils [Accessed April 1, 2015].

[63] Mother Nature Network, *15 Animals that are Living Fossils,* http://www.mnn.com/earth-matters/animals/photos/15-animals-that-are-living-fossils/from-another-era. [Accessed April 1, 2015].

dinosaurs and the evidence of catastrophism, the Cambrian explosion, and living fossils. All of these lines of evidence are compelling for making the case that there are better explanations than what mainstream science has provided to account for their existence. If we are looking at identifying God, these evidences are not sufficient within themselves. If we are to take the God of the Bible seriously we must account for the lack of fossil evidence concerning humans within the geologic column. After all, the Bible tells us that humans and land animals were created on the same day of the week and only a day apart from birds and fish. If this is true, why are we told by mainstream science that there is no evidence of humans in the fossil record?

The irony of this is that there have been humans found in the deeper strata of the fossil record; humans that resemble modern humans to boot. There are several big examples of such fossils throughout the world but before diving into this information, it needs to be made clear that human fossils are not the only rarity in the fossil record. Vertebrates, in general comprise no more than 1/100 of 1% the fossil record. One might question why humans are such a rare find in the fossil record, but then we also must ask why all vertebrates that are found are so rare within the layers of the earth.

As stated earlier, fossilization is a rare phenomenon and most vertebrates live significantly above the ocean floor. Many invertebrates live deep in the ocean. It makes sense that such creatures would appear in abundance in the fossil record while vertebrates are rare. What could make humans a more difficult find is the fact that they are smarter than the average land animal. They would have a better understanding of how to seek refuge in the midst of this catastrophic flood.

Some of the most incredible human fossils are in in La Sal, Utah. Inside of a coal mine in La Sal, Utah bones of humans were discovered that are found in the same layer of strata as many dinosaurs. The evolutionist community scoffed at these bones, all the while not denying their existence. They claimed that they could have been a result of a mine collapse or a person falling into a pit. Despite the fact that little can be done to refute these arguments, there is no evidence to support these claims either. The bones are well defined, fully formed, and are virtually identical to modern humans. Had these been the bones of dinosaurs there would be no dispute concerning how old the bones should be. It seems creationists have not lost sleep over the scientific community's disagreement concerning the understanding of these bones. Most creationists know that faith is not dependent on fossils. They are also aware that the world is littered with evidence of human remains in the same strata as dinosaurs.[64]

Although the La Sal, Utah remains are exciting, human footprints are considered to be the best evidence for mankind's existence deep in the fossil record. The most noted are those that once existed at the Paluxy River in Texas. In this sample it was discovered that human footprints were found in the same strata as dinosaur footprints.[65,66] The evolutionary community did not know how to react to this discovery either. Their first reaction was to say that the footprints were carved. After running several tests on the footprints it was discovered that they were not carved. Then it was thought that they were a result of erosion. More testing confirmed that they were not formed through erosion. Next, it was proposed that maybe certain dinosaurs had human-like feet. The suggestion was laughable but

---

[64] Don Patton, *The Record of the Rocks Part 1*, http://www.bible.ca/tracks/video/don-patton-evolution-refuted-creation-science-flood-geology-record-of-the-rocks.htm. [Accessed April 1, 2015].

[65] Elizabeth Mitchel, *Paluxy River Tracks in Texas Spotlight*, April 14, 2014. https://answersingenesis.org/dinosaurs/footprints/paluxy-river-tracks-in-texas-spotlight/ [Accessed April 1, 2015].

[66] Morris, 329-330.

there was no evidence to would suggest that they were wrong. After further investigation, it was discovered that these tracks were actually inside of fossilized dinosaur footprints. The evolutionary community decided that these tracks must have been made by dinosaurs and coincidentally these human-like tracks resulted from gradual erosion. Possible, but the footprints of the humans were very distinct and very detailed. Finally, one scientist figured it out. Aliens came along and made the footprints 65 million years ago. Dr. Don Patton, one of the defenders of these footprints, responded to this suggestion by asking what a super-advanced culture that traveled light years to get to earth were doing running around barefoot in the mud. His scientist friend did not care much for that response.[67]

It should be very clear to anybody who gives a fair hearing of the evidence that there is plenty of support for a global flood. This brief look at some of the fossil evidence barely scratches the surface of the sum total of all of the evidence at our disposal. For some of you, this evidence is totally new and I would encourage you to investigate it yourself. The creationist perspective on this evidence is controversial and highly disputed but I believe it is superior to its alternative. There is so much evidence within geology to support a global flood that it is irrefutable proof of creation.

---

[67] Don Patton, *The Record of the Rocks Part 1*.

MANKIND

So God created man in his own image,
in the image of God he created him;
male and female he created them.
~Genesis 1:27

What is a human life worth? Can it be quantified by a dollar amount? Are some people worth more than others? Mankind is a truly unique creation. Unique in that it has yearnings for ideals that are too abstract for the animal kingdom to grasp. We yearn for justice, purpose, and love. We could go into a more scientific discussion about the uniqueness of mankind, but doing so would actually trivialize what it is that makes humanity an extra-natural creation. Mankind was created in the image of God.

The Greek creation myth reminds us of the uniqueness of mankind in the midst of the animal kingdom. It was the Titan Epimetheus who took upon the task of creating life. Every group of animal had its unique gift. Birds could fly, fish could swim, and others could burrow into the ground. Predators were given sharp claws and big teeth, while their prey was given defensive mechanisms like horns and shells. Epimetheus then remembered that he needed to create man. The thing about Epimetheus is that he always gets ahead of himself. His name actually means *afterthought.* After creating the animals, Epimetheus realized that he had not saved any gifts for humans.

He ran to his brother, Prometheus for some wise assistance. Prometheus, whose name means *forethought,* analyzed the situation and then gave man something far greater than any gift in the animal kingdom. He gave them the very power of the gods. He gave them fire. He stole the fire straight from the sun, Zeus' armory. When Zeus saw the flames of man lighting the dark world he became furious. He found Prometheus, bound him up, and tortured him. In Zeus' opinion, mankind had become far too arrogant and had to be dealt with.

In response he plotted a fate for mankind far worse than that of Prometheus. He created a sinister being whose evil knows no end. You might be familiar with this creation from other creation stories. This entity would entice man, cause him turmoil, and usher into the world the plagues of death and suffering. Such evil had never been known. Even the evil the gods faced in their war with the Titans would pale in comparison to this most formidable of foes. Zeus punished man with his most dastardly creation of all: woman – uh, I mean, umm, [gulp]. Feel free to ignore the last few sentences. Up until the creation of woman (which is actually a very lovely description in the Greek myth), this story is incredible. It exemplifies how man is not like the animals. Yes, in some ways mankind seems at a disadvantage to the animals. But it has at its disposal a glimpse of eternity; a divine essence which is a far greater advantage and blessing than any of the gifts of the animals.

In the Bible, King David knew the place of man in relation to God. In Psalm 8, through beauty and wonder, he describes the relationship between God and man:

> When I consider your heavens,
> The work of your fingers,
> What is man that you are mindful of him,
> the son of man that you care for him?
> You made him a little lower than the heavenly beings
> and crowned him with glory and honor.

God makes it clear from the very first chapter of the Bible that mankind is a special creation. He took five full days before creating it to build an environment in which humans could flourish. People were meant to be the Creator's representation on planet earth. Theologians refer to humanity as the *imago dei* or the *image of God* because God said that it was in his image that he created men and women. It is sad to see mankind in the state that it exists today with crime, murder, lies, adultery, idolatry, and so forth. Humans were always meant to be an innocent creation that did only good for the world. Even though people have strayed far from God, it gave the LORD an opportunity to prove his love for the entire human race.

It is odd to think that all of the suffering and death that the world faces is due to the disobedience of humans. In the Garden of Eden, God gave mankind a choice. They could either avoid the Tree of Knowledge of Good and Evil and live forever in paradise, or choose to eat its fruit and die. Mankind chose to eat from the tree and reaped the consequences. Over time, humanity has drifted further and further from God. It was not too long before people became hostile to God.

Granted the ever widening gap between mankind and God, there was still something there that resonated with the human heart. Because we have been created in God's image, we have an intrinsic sense of purpose. We seek to live meaningful lives because deep down we know that we were created for a reason. We also have a strong desire to see justice enacted in this present world. It is only right that people be treated fair and that those who are wrong would be compensated according to the degree of the offense. Despite our desire for justice we also know that love is greater than justice. Justice divvies out consequences where love shows mercy. Even though someone might wrong us or offend us, we choose to remain gracious because we know that in an eternal perspective we deserve no better than God's judgment, yet he forgave us.

The Bible is clear that Jesus Christ, even when mankind was an enemy of God, died for the sins of the entire world. In this righteous act God proved his love because everyone who has ever lived deserved the punishment due for sin. The Son of God chose to take the punishment of sin upon himself so that people would be made right in the eyes of God. Through believing in God's only Son, Jesus, mankind is given the opportunity to be born of the Holy Spirit into God's family. It is no wonder that the Bible tells us that we love him because he first loved us, for his standard of righteousness and love is far beyond our capacity as mere mortals.

It is the incredible fact that mankind was created in God's image that we are all evidence that the world was created. We are a diamond in the rough. It is true that we are not necessarily good in all that we do, but no other animal can tend to the world as we do, nor can any animal destroy the world as well as we can. It is through Jesus Christ, God's Son, that we truly know our worth as humans because he died for each and every one of us.

CONCLUSION

After examining these ten proofs for creation it should be easy to conclude that God created the universe. Nothing within the universe contradicts the notion that all things were created by God and designed with a purpose. Each proof collaborates perfectly with the others to reveal the reality of a supernatural Creator who structured the universe, constructed the earth, and designed the intricacies of life. Let us review the ten proofs:

- The First Law of Thermodynamics makes it clear that under natural circumstances matter cannot be created or destroyed. In order for the universe to exist, a supernatural source would need to intervene.

- The Second Law of Thermodynamics establishes that the Big Bang and evolution could never happen because all things trend toward a more disorderly state. Evolution would violate this law.

- The Expanding Universe implies that the universe had a starting point. The universe could not begin on its own accord but requires God to set things in motion.

- The Anthropic Principle is scientific evidence that the universe was designed for life.

- DNA poses many problems for the theory of evolution. Some have even referred to the incredible information stored inside of DNA as the signature in the cell, referring to a Creator.

- Biological Predestination shows that the existence of life came about intentionally, not on accident.

- Irreducible Complexity is strong evidence that certain systems could never evolve. The only likely alternative would require a Designer.

- Natural Selection has shown that there is no evidence for macro-evolution. On the same token, it operates on the principle that all creatures procreate after their own kinds, just as the Bible tells us.

- Evidence for the Global Flood is overwhelming when it is given a fair look. If this evidence is taken seriously, it is clear that the ancient world was correct in their assertion that there was a global flood. The Bible's flood story seems to account for all of the flood evidence better than any other account.

- Mankind is incredible proof of creation. Having been created in God's image it is clear that there is no creature like mankind.

There are other proofs of creation but all of the evidence in the world is not enough to convince one who has a closed mind. Jesus once said that even if one were be to raised from the dead, that would not be enough to convince certain people.[68] In Ravi Zacharias' book, *The End of Reason,* he wrote,

> *The problem with evidence is that it is very much limited to the moment and creates the demand for more evidence...The worldview of the Christian faith is simple enough. God has put enough into this world to make faith in him the most reasonable thing. But he has*

[68] Luke 16:31

left enough out to make it impossible to live by sheer reason alone.[69]

Many people have rejected sound reasons for believing in God. But, as Ravi Zacharias points out, a lack of faith can override the evidence. There are 10 evidences listed in this book that prove creation. The facts speak for themselves that a very powerful designer created everything in existence.

All that is left to do, is to believe. The God of the Bible is both far and near. Far, in that we are separated from him by a chasm of sin. Near, in that he reconciled us to himself through the blood of his Son, Jesus Christ. The ten proofs cannot convert you to the truth. They are merely a beacon to guide you. Jesus is the Son of God and only through him can you experience eternal life.

If you need to, investigate the evidence further. Look to see what the opposition has to say about the ten proofs in which I have exposed. Critically analyze what other works have to say, and then measure it against the best counterarguments, as well. Even if you find their evidence more convincing, examine

---

[69] Ravi Zacharias, *The End of Reason,* (Zondervan, Grand Rapids Michigan, 2008), 75.

the life of Jesus Christ. Ask yourself if anything else could account for the movement that he created. Was he just a man who had a controversial message or was he the Son of God, who was destined to be crucified and raised back to life after three days to save you and to save me? Does He present that evidence to you today?

ABOUT THE AUTHOR

Bill Seng earned his Bachelor's in Health Science from Cleveland State University in 2007 and his Master's of Divinity from Winebrenner Theological Seminary in 2011. Currently, he works for Marathon Petroleum Company as a Technical Writer and writes a weekly blog post for the Worldview Warriors that can be found at www.worldviewwarriors.org. He and his wife, Melissa, are entrepreneurs and enjoy building their business together. They have both been blessed with their son, Jaden, who was born in August of 2013.

References

Answers in Genesis. *Fruit Flies and Advantageous Mutations*. 2010, https://answersingenesis.org/genetics/mutations/fruit-flies-advantageous-mutations/ [Accessed March 31, 2015].

Astronomy 161 The Solar System. *The Universe of Aristotle and Ptolemy*. http://csep10.phys.utk.edu/astr161/lect/retrograde/aristotle.html [April 1, 2015].

Behe, Michael J. *Darwin's Black Box*. 2006 Free Press: New York.

Biography.com website. *Galileo*. 2015. http://www.biography.com/people/galileo-9305220#death-and- legacy [Accessed April 2, 2015].

Carnegie Institution for Science. *1917: Albert Einstein Invents the Cosmological Constant*. https://cosmology.carnegiescience.edu/timeline/1917 [Accessed April 2, 2015].

Choi, Charles Q. *Asteroid Impact That Killed the Dinosaurs: New Evidence*. 2015. Livescience. http://www.livescience.com/26933-

chicxulubcosmic-impact-dinosaurs.html [Accessed   April 1, 2015].

Evolution News and Views. *Darwin's Finches Show Rule-Constrained Variation in Beak Size.* 2010. http://www.evolutionnews.org/2014/06/darwins_finches086581.html) [April 2,   2015].

Faulkner, Danny. *Study Says Universe had No Beginning and No Big Bang?* 2015. Answers in Genesis https://answersingenesis.org/big-bang/study-says-universe-had-no-beginning/ [Accessed April 1, 2015].

Gates, Bill. 1995. *The Good Road Ahead.* Penguin Books: New York. http://www.goodreads.com/quotes/336336-dna-is-like-a-computer-program-but-far-far- more [Accessed April 2, 2015].

Genetics Home Reference. *What is DNA?* 2015. http://ghr.nlm.nih.gov/handbook/basics/dna [Accessed April 2, 2015].

George B. Johnson, Jonathan B. Losos, Peter H. Raven, and Susan R. Singer 2005. *Biology, 7th ed.* Madison, Wisconsin: McGraw Hill Higher Education.

Giancoli, Douglas C. 2005. *Physics*. Upper Saddle River, New Jersey: Pearson Prentice Hall.

Globe Urban Internet Solutions. *A Brief History of Bison.* Bisonbasics.com. http://www.bisonbasics.com/history/past_future.html [Accessed April 1, 2015].

Hall, Stephen S. *Hidden Treasures in Junk DNA*. 2012. Scientific American. http://www.scientificamerican.com/article/hidden-treasures-in-junk-dna/[Accessed April 2, 2015].

Hames, David. 2006. *Incredible Creatures that Defy Evolution, vol. 1.* Exploration Films, Reel Productions: Rockwall, Texas.

Heger, Monica. *What is a Theory?* 2012. Livescience. http://www.livescience.com/32390-what- is-a-theory.html [Accessed April 1, 2015].

Holt, Jim. *Why Does the Universe Exist?* 2014.TED. https://www.ted.com/talks/ jim_holt_why_does_the_universe_exist?language=en

Hubble Site. *Discovering Planets Beyond: Alien Atmospheres.* http://hubblesite.org/hubble_discoveries/discov

ering_planets_beyond/alien-atmospheres [Accessed April 2, 2015].

Institute for Creation Research. *Living Fossils Display No Evidence of Evolution's Long Ages.* http://www.icr.org/living-fossils [Accessed April 1, 2015].

J. D. Myers and Phil Newman. *Starchild Question of the Month for February 2013.* 2013. NASA. http://starchild.gsfc.nasa.gov/docs/StarChild/questions/question54.html [Accessed April 1, 2015].

Johnson, Nat and Natural History Magazine (producers). *Blind Evolution or Intelligent Design?* 2002. National Center for Science Education: The American Museum of Natural History. https://www.youtube.com/watch?v=CmMVgOTCukQ [Accessed March 31, 2015].

Kenyon, Dean H. 1969. *Biochemical Predestination.* McGraw-Hill: New York.

Krauss, Lawrence. Think Twice. *Science Refutes God.* 2012. Intelligence squared. http://intelligencesquaredus.org/debates/past-debates/item/728-science-refutes-god [Accessed March 30, 2015].

Luskin, Casey. *Erwin and Valentine's The Cambrian Explosion Affirms Major Points in Darwin's Doubt: The Cambrian Enigma is Unresolved.* 2013. Evolution News and Views. http://www.evolutionnews.org/2013/06/erwin_valentine_cambrian_explosion0736 71. html [Accessed April 1, 2015].

Lyell, Charles. 1997. *Principles of Geology.* Penguin Books: New York.

McIntosh, Andy. *Just Add Energy...* 2007. Answers in Genesis. https://answersingenesis.org/physics/just-add-energy/ [Accessed April 1, 2015].

Matthew, Patrick. 1831. *Naval Timber and Arboriculture.* Neil & Co. Printers: Edinburgh.

Meyer, Angela. *The World of Whales.* 1996. https://answersingenesis.org/aquatic-animals/the-world-of-whales/ [Accessed April 1, 2015].

Meyer, Stephen. 2014. *Signature in the Cell.* New York: HarperOne. https://www.youtube.com/watch?v=TVkdQhNdzHU [Accessed March 31, 2015].

Michael Crichton and Steven Spielberg. 1993. *Jurassic Park.* Universal Pictures.

Mitchell, Elizabeth. *Cambrian Explosion or Creation Week – Key to Vertebrate Success.* 2015. Answers in Genesis. https://answersingenesis.org/theory-of-evolution/evolution- timeline/cambrian-explosion-or-creation-week-key-to-vertebrate-success/ [Accessed April 1, 2015].

Mitchel, Elizabeth. *Paluxy River Tracks in Texas Spotligh.* 2014. Answers in Genesis. https://answersingenesis.org/dinosaurs/footprints/paluxy-river-tracks-in-texas-spotlight/ [Accessed April 1, 2015].

Mitchell, Tommy. *The Second Law of Thermodynamics Began at the Fall.* 2010. Answers in Genesis. https://answersingenesis.org/creationism/arguments-to-avoid/the-second-law-of-thermodynamics-began-at-the-fall/ [Accessed April 1, 2015]

Morris, Henry. 2008. *The Biblical Basis for Modern Science.* Master Books: Green Forest, Arkansas.

Mosher, Dave. *Gorillas More Related to People Than Thought, Genome Says.* 2012. http://news.nationalgeographic.com/news/2012/03/120306-gorilla-genome-apes-humans-evolution-science/ [Accessed March 31, 2015].

Morris, John D. *What Distinguishes Man From Ape?* Institute for Creation Research. http://www.icr.org/article/what-distinguishes-man-from-ape [Accessed April 1, 2015].

Moskowitz, Clara. *Einstein's Biggest Blunder Turns Out to be Right*. 2010. Space.com. http://www.space.com/9593-einstein-biggest-blunder-turns.html. [Accessed April 2, 2015].

Mother Nature Network. *15 Animals that are Living Fossils.* http://www.mnn.com/earth-matters/animals/photos/15-animals-that-are-living-fossils/from-another-era. [Accessed April 1, 2015].

NASA. *Mars, Water, and Life*. http://mars.jpl.nasa.gov/msp98/why.html [Accessed April 2, 2015].

National Oceanic and Atmospheric Association. *Tsunami.* http://www.tsunami.noaa.gov/ [Accessed April 1, 2015].

Patton, Don. *The Record of the Rocks Part 1*, http://www.bible.ca/tracks/video/don-patton-evolution-refuted-creation-science-flood-geology-record-of-the-rocks.htm. [Accessed April 1, 2015].

Purdom, Georgia. 2007. *The Code of Life.* St. Petersburg, Kentucky: Answers in Genesis.

Redd, Nola Taylor. *What is Dark Matter?* May 1, 2013. Space.com. http://www.space.com/20930-dark-matter.html [Accessed March 31, 2015].

Science Made Simple, *The Scientific Method by Science Made Simple.* 2014. http://www.sciencemadesimple.com/scientific_method.html#experiment [Accessed April 1, 2015].

Siepel, Adam. *Darwinian Alchemy, 2015: Human genes from noncoding DNA.* Cold Spring Harbor. http://genome.cshlp.org/content/19/10/1693.full.html [Accessed April 2, 2015].

Snelling, Andrew. *What Are Some of the Best Flood Evidences?* 2015. https://answersingenesis.org/the-flood/what-are-some-of-the-best-flood-evidences/ [Accessed April 2, 2015].

Strobel, Lee. 2004. *The Case for a Creator.* Zondervan : Grand Rapids, Michigan.

Susman, Art.*Our Planet.* http://www.mcc.cmu.ac.th/graduate/Agro723/R

eading_Materials/Our_Planet/ Planet.html [Accessed April 1, 2015].

Taylor, Ian. 2003. *In the Minds of Men: Darwin and the New World Order, fifth edition.* TFE Publishing: Zimmerman, Minnesota. http://www.creationism.org/books/ TaylorInMindsMen\TaylorIMMe05.htm[Accessed March 31, 2015].

Thompson, Bert. *So Long Eternal Universe; "Hello Beginning, Hello End!"* 2003. Apologetics Press. http://www.apologeticspress.org/apcontent.aspx?category=12&article=310

Tompkins, Jeffery P. *RNA Editing: Biocomplexity hits a new high.* 2015. Institute for Creation Research. http://www.icr.org/article/8649 [Accessed April 2, 2015].

Truth in Science. *Darwin's Finches.* 2013. http://www.truthinscience.org.uk/tis2/index.php/evidence-for-evolution-mainmenu-65/53-darwins-finches.html [April 2, 2015].

Warner, Carl. *Evolution: The Grand Experiment.* 2014. http://www.thegrandexperiment.com/whale-evolution.html [Accessed April 1, 2015].

Weisstein, Eric. *Copernicus, Nicholaus (1474-1543)*. 2007. http://scienceworld.wolfram.com/biography/Copernicus.html [Accessed April 1, 2015].

W. Peter Allen and Stephen C. Meyer (writers), James W. Adams (executive producer), Lad Allen (director). 2010. *Unlocking the Mystery of Life*. La Mirada, California: Illustra Media.

Zacharias, Ravi. 2008. *The End of Reason.* Zondervan: Grand Rapids, Michigan.

Zhang, Jianzhi. *Evolution by Gene Duplication: An Update*. 2003. Trends in Ecology and Evolution vol. 18 No. 6. http://www.umich.edu/~zhanglab/publications/2003/Zhang_2003_TIG_18_292.pdf [Accessed April 2, 2015].

Bill Seng

Made in the USA
Charleston, SC
04 July 2015